Nineteenth-Century European Civilization 1815-1914

GEOFFREY BRUUN

LONDON
OXFORD UNIVERSITY PRESS
NEW YORK   TORONTO
1959

Oxford University Press, Amen House, London E.C.4
GLASGOW NEW YORK TORONTO MELBOURNE WELLINGTON
BOMBAY CALCUTTA MADRAS KARACHI KUALA LUMPUR
CAPE TOWN IBADAN NAIROBI ACCRA

First published in The European Inheritance,
1954, and included in The Home University
Library, *1959*

Printed in Great Britain by
Butler & Tanner Ltd., Frome and London

THE HOME UNIVERSITY LIBRARY
OF MODERN KNOWLEDGE

239

NINETEENTH-CENTURY
EUROPEAN CIVILIZATION

EDITOR OF
The Home University Library
of Modern Knowledge
SIR GEORGE CLARK, D. LITT., F.B.A.

Books on European History
in the Home University Library

No. 13 MEDIEVAL EUROPE
(H. W. C. DAVIS)

No. 232 EARLY MODERN EUROPE
from about 1450 to about 1720
(SIR GEORGE CLARK)

No. 228 WORLD HISTORY
from 1914 to 1950
(DAVID THOMSON)

PREFACE

IN European history the period between the battle of Waterloo in 1815 and the opening of the First World War in 1914 has a discernible unity and these dates provide the logical though not the strictly chronological limits for a discussion of European civilization in the nineteenth century. By 1815 that civilization had already exerted a profound and increasing influence on the other continents. As the activities of the European peoples between 1815 and 1914 were not limited to Europe, it is necessary, in evaluating them, to take account of Europe's global influence and the reciprocal effects of European expansion.

The six chapters that follow are arranged in chronological sequence with the period of years covered by each designated in its title. For additional reference it may be noted that all major entries in the index are followed by their dates.

These chapters were first published (1954) as section six of *The European Inheritance*, edited by Sir Ernest Barker, Sir George Clark, and Professor Paul Vaucher. It is a special pleasure to acknowledge my debt to them and to the editors of the Oxford University Press for their helpful suggestions and perceptive criticism.

Ithaca, New York   G. B.

16 July 1958

CONTENTS

INTRODUCTION

THE nineteenth century was the great age of European expansion. For 300 years, following the voyages of Columbus, Da Gama, and Magellan, the shadow of the European hegemony had been moving across the oceans. For ten generations hardy explorers, traders, and colonizers had been hoisting sail in the harbours of the Old World to lay the broad foundation for empires overseas. Not until the nineteenth century, however, when western science 'put a girdle round about the earth', did the Europeans come into the plenitude of their imperial heritage. Their aggressive superiority and spectacular conquests eclipsed all historical prologues, though limited precedents might be found, for instance, in the spread of Hellenistic culture after the fourth century B.C. But Hellenistic civilization was circumscribed by its Mediterranean environment, whereas the hegemony of the modern Europeans expanded until all the continents of the earth yielded them some form of advantage. Between 1815 and 1914 the world entered a new era of global integration under the compulsion of western technology, an era that might, without undue exaggeration, be termed the European age. Before the nineteenth century closed European civilization dominated or impinged upon every segment of the globe, and all important groups of the world's population had taken the imprint of occidental culture or endured its pressure.

For the peoples of Europe the period between 1815 and 1914 was an era of such remarkable progress at home that it half-blinded them to the ever widening influence of their economy overseas. It was a period unmarred by any long or seriously debilitating wars, a century during which the cumulative energies of Europe could be turned to constructive enterprises, and surplus capital and population could find profitable outlets in other continents. Each generation enjoyed an increase in wealth and comfort, a widening of economic opportunity, an improvement in the standards of nutrition, health, and sanitation. With each decade new advances in technology speeded the mechanization of industry, new cities reared their anarchic skylines, new levels of production were attained in the factories and the mills. But the most significant indexes of progress were neither political nor economic; they were demographic. Throughout the nineteenth century the population of Europe increased at an average of three-fourths per cent. per year, a ratio of growth never before sustained by so vast a population for so long a period.

This phenomenal growth of population was a major clue to the European supremacy. General estimates agree that the population of Europe in 1815 was about 200,000,000; the nineteenth century saw this figure more than double, to reach a total of 460,000,000 by 1914. Other continents also recorded an exceptional rise in numbers during the same span of years, but the Europeans did better than hold their own. In 1815 the people living within the geographical confines of Europe constituted perhaps one-fifth of the world total; by 1914 they constituted one-fourth. To realize the singular nature of this triumph it should be noted that all the rival continents had a higher general birth-rate than nineteenth-century Europe. The Europeans altered the demographic balance of the globe, not by raising their birth-rate, but by lowering their death-rate.

The figures for Europe alone, however, fail to suggest the full scope of the European achievement in population growth. Between the fall of Napoleon in 1815 and the outbreak of the First World War in 1914 more than 40,000,000 emigrants left their European homes to settle in other continents. The consequences of this vast migration made the Europeans in large measure an extra-European stock. In 1815 there were less than 20,000,000 people of European birth or predominantly European blood beyond the seas. By 1914 the total had multiplied tenfold to almost 200,000,000.

This increase and dispersal of the Europeans during the nineteenth century was a fitting reflection of their imperial mood. By 1914 there were as many people of European descent outside Europe as there had been inside Europe a century earlier. Or, to state the fact another way, by 1914 one European in three was living overseas. As already noted, the 460,000,000 people in Europe at that date comprised one-fourth of the world population. If some 200,000,000 people of European blood living abroad are added, it becomes clear that there were nearly 700,000,000 people of European descent in 1914. The racial stock of this smallest of the continents, including its emigrant sons and their descendants, had come to constitute one-third of the human race.

Statistics such as these make it clear that a balanced chronicle of nineteenth-century Europe must transcend the narrow limits of the European stage. The major scenes of the drama were still enacted there, but the focus had widened to include a *magna Europa* beyond the seas. The day was definitely past when colonial annals could be treated as an epilogue to European events. The political ties that had once bound the New World to the Old were severed or slackened by 1815. Cities in the wilderness had grown to sovereign stature and become the nuclei of independent nations. Yet even the remotest frontier communities founded by European initiative knew themselves the offshoots of a living parent culture, as their nostalgic names so often testified. Their traditions and their techniques could be traced across the seas and down the centuries; their roots reached back to medieval monasteries that once dotted the expanding rim of Christendom; their defences recalled the Roman camps that marked the borders of an earlier *imperium*. By the nineteenth century the far-flung colonies of the Old World were rising to maturity as dominions or republics, but they were still the custodians of a common civilization and heirs of the European inheritance.

In the pages that follow the adventures of these European peoples overseas will be traced step by step with those of the Old World nations. The influence of Europe upon the world had been from the first an interdependent, a reciprocal process. As the Atlantic community evolved, European civilization became something vast and vague for which no satisfactory name could be found; but the spirit of this common western culture set the pattern of development in regions even more remote, in South Africa, Australasia, and the Far East. Upon Europe itself the exportation of ideas and techniques, of capital and population, had a continuous and increasing effect throughout the nineteenth century. The heavy investment of European capital helped to develop the resources of other continents and made Europe in a sense 'the world's banker', while the competition of the European powers for concessions and territory in Africa and Asia sometimes intensified local European tensions. The history of nineteenth-century Europe became a drama of rising pressures and competing policies that mounted to a climax within the framework of a precarious equilibrium. It was the fate of the twentieth century to inherit the violent and tragic denouement of these accelerating drives.

Europe

in 1815

Chapter One

POLITICAL REACTION AND ECONOMIC PROGRESS (1815–30)

The year 1815 rather than 1800 is the logical threshold to nineteenth-century Europe. The shocks of the French Revolution and the Napoleonic wars had cracked the rigid institutions of the old régime. When the tremors and the hammering subsided, the Europeans found themsevles living in reconstructed quarters, half-ancient, half-impoverished, but with an ampler frame and more spacious corridors than the cramped architecture they had outgrown. The statesmen of the Restoration era, who repaired the shaken structure after Napoleon's fall, have been accused of planning for the past rather than the future of European society. It is a charge which liberal historians, wise after the event, often delighted to emphasize, but it is a charge that ignores almost entirely the mood and purport of the Restoration settlement.

For the reactionary statesmen who converged on Vienna in 1814 for probate of the revolutionary testament were neither antiquarians nor prophets; they were harassed diplomats bedevilled by the imperious problems of the present. Their object was to re-establish peace after a quarter of a century of arbitrary political engineering and almost incessant warfare; and they decided, humanly enough, that security might best be

sought by invoking the counter-revolutionary principles of political immobility and dynastic permanence.
Wherever old landmarks survived and could serve a
useful purpose, they repaired them. But their basic aim
was to restore not the injustices of the old régime but
its remembered virtues, above all the benefits of stable
government and the security of a state system in
reasonable equilibrium.

Judged by these sober aims the diplomats who drafted
the Vienna treaties were statesmen of ability. The
general settlement that they devised was subsequently
modified in detail, but for a hundred years it was altered
within the orbit of their cautious formulas. The peace
congress had been called, as its secretary Friedrich
Gentz acknowledged, to divide among the victors the
spoils taken from the vanquished, a delicate operation
which it executed with due regard for reciprocal compensation and without unnecessary rancour or vin-
dictiveness. After 1815 the great powers avoided an
appeal to the sword for almost forty years; and when
wars came they were wars for limited objectives, conflicts that could be localized and that were never permitted to reach ruinous and exhausting proportions. In
spite of numerous defects the Vienna settlement can be
seen in perspective as the portal to a century of progress,
stability, and expansion. It opened the longest period
unmarred by a general war that Europe had known
since the Roman peace of the first and second centuries
of the Christian era.

The pattern of European history after 1815 depended
upon the interplay of three major factors, one political,

B

one naval, and one economic. The political factor was
the temporary ascendency of the four victorious powers,
Britain, Austria, Russia, and Prussia. With France in
eclipse these 'Big Four' were in a position to redraft the
map of Europe in almost any form they could agree on
as mutually acceptable. The second factor, equally significant in shaping any realistic settlement, was the naval
supremacy of Great Britain. Nowhere on the globe was
there a navy or an alliance of naval forces strong enough
to defy the British mastery of the seas. The third factor,
less obvious to most European diplomats, but potentially the most powerful of all as an arbiter of European
destiny, was the mechanization of industry. The 'dark
Satanic mills' were about to release their rhythmic
energies, and the steam-engine was waiting to transform
European economic life. To assess the influence of these
three factors is far from easy, and the method adopted
here will be to consider them individually in the order
named.

The political reconstruction of the Continent was of
primary concern to the governments of Austria, Russia,
and Prussia. Austria, four times defeated by Napoleon's
smashing campaigns, showed a surprising power of
recuperation; and the selection of Vienna for the peace
congress was a tribute to this revived prestige. The
choice was also a tribute to the enterprise of Klemens
von Metternich, the Austrian foreign minister, who displayed his social and diplomatic talents as cicerone to
the assembled delegates. Metternich believed himself
predestined 'to prop a falling house', and he feared with
reason that the Habsburg realm would disintegrate if

the national and liberal tides stirred up by the French Revolution rose again to inundate Europe. The empire on the Danube had become an historical anachronism in an age of national states; for although its area and population made Austria a great power, its society remained feudal and aristocratic and its disparate segments included Germans, Magyars, Poles, Czechs, Croats, Italians, and several lesser minorities. Yet the tincture of tradition was strong, the dynastic pride of the Habsburgs even stronger, and the collapse of the French *imperium* left Austria the predestined champion of the conservative forces. When Vienna played host to Europe in 1814–15 the receptions were as brilliant, the music as seductive, the women as beautiful, and the prestige of the Austrian court apparently as unassailable as ever. The Habsburg empire entered its final century in the golden glow of a St. Martin's summer that seemed like the return of spring.

Externally at least, Austria appeared little changed by the rude shocks of the revolutionary age. The distant Belgian provinces (the Austrian Netherlands) were permanently lost, but as compensation the Habsburgs kept the territories of the late Venetian Republic and the province of Lombardy. The Holy Roman Empire was not revived (that archaic fiction had been dissolved in 1806), but Austria assumed the lead in a new diplomatic creation, the German Confederation. This was a loose league of thirty-eight German states the governments of which sent delegates to a diet that met at Frankfort-on-the-Main. Hopes for more liberal institutions and a closer national union, which had fired many

German hearts in the fervour of the *Freiheitskrieg*, were frustrated by this feeble compromise. Although the charter of the German Confederation promised 'a representative form of government' to the component states, Austrian pressure nullified this provision in action.

Prussia, like Austria, regained lost prestige at Vienna, and the territorial bargaining added part of Saxony and all of Swedish Pomerania to the Hohenzollern possessions. But the war efforts against the French had overtaxed the limited resources of the Prussian state, necessitating a decade or more of convalescence. So Prussia followed a cautious policy of retrenchment and recuperation after 1815, while Austria dictated to the lesser German states and set the tone of central European politics.

Russian interests were championed at Vienna by the Tsar Alexander I in person. The personality of this 'crowned Hamlet' whom Napoleon characterized as a 'shifty Byzantine' baffled his contemporaries. It seemed incongruous that an autocrat of all the Russias should harbour genuinely liberal sentiments; yet Alexander had argued against hereditary monarchy with Napoleon, and he solicited information on the United States Constitution from Thomas Jefferson when the word republic was anathema to his princely colleagues. In the Tsar's heart the impulses of a humanitarian warred with the calculations of a statesman, and as late as 1820 he still dreamed of a liberal constitution for Russia. But the tug of tradition proved too strong, reaction triumphed, and after Alexander's death in 1825 his brother Nicholas I assured Metternich that no more flashes of mystical liberalism would confuse the eastern European horizon.

Tsarist Russia, like Austria and Prussia, had little to gain and much to lose if the revolutionary tide rose again. The hereditary monarchs at St. Petersburg Vienna, and Berlin were tacitly united by similar interests and problems, for all had discontented minorities to control and all held segments of the dismembered Polish state. The 'fourth partition' of Poland, consummated at Vienna, allotted the lion's share to Russia, and Alexander created a constitutional Polish kingdom with himself as king. Since he also retained Finland, which his armies had overrun in 1809, and Bessarabia, which had been acquired from the Turks in 1812, Russia emerged from the revolutionary wars with more extensive conquests than any other continental power.

While the representatives of the 'Big Four' sat behind closed doors, subdividing Europe, the delegates of the secondary states haunted the antechambers. They knew that the fate of the smaller nations depended on two issues: the desire to penalize those princes who had remained loyal to Napoleon overlong, and the desire to 'contain' France in future by blocking the likelier points of French expansion. Thus Denmark forfeited Norway, with its million inhabitants, to Sweden, the latter having possessed the foresight to desert the French cause early in 1812. Saxony, elevated to the status of a kingdom by Napoleon, lost two-fifths of its territory to Prussia. To block French expansion in the north-east three million Belgians and over two million Dutch were placed under the rule of William I of the

house of Orange, to form the kingdom of the United
Netherlands. In the south-east a possible revival of
French pressure was countered by guaranteeing the in-
dependence of Switzerland, and by strengthening the
kingdom of Piedmont–Sardinia, where the house of
Savoy was restored and granted the late republic of
Genoa as an additional make-weight. Republics were
definitely out of fashion with the peacemakers of 1815.
Lombardy and Venetia became Habsburg provinces; at
Naples a Bourbon claimant, Ferdinand I, was enthroned
as King of the Two Sicilies; while in central Italy the
papal states came once more under the temporal rule of
Pope Pius VII. The principle of legitimacy likewise
triumphed in the Iberian peninsula, Ferdinand VII
regaining the Spanish throne and Portugal submitting
to the house of Braganza.

The outstanding vindication of legitimacy, however,
was the return of Louis XVIII to Paris, where he proclaimed his anxiety to re-weld the chain of time, broken
by that 'fatal interlude', the French Revolution. The
imperturbable Talleyrand, who had deserted Napoleon
and rallied to the Bourbons, appeared at Vienna as the
plenipotentiary of Louis XVIII, with legitimacy as his
trump card. It would, he persuaded the 'Big Four', be
a contradiction of principle to offer Louis XVIII a
truncated kingdom: France must be restored to the
Bourbons intact. The unexpected escape of Napoleon
from his exile on Elba, and his brief recovery of power
during the 'Hundred Days', proved that many Frenchmen were far from repentant, and this 'last flight of the
eagle' stirred the Allies to a sterner mood. After Water-

loo Napoleon was dispatched to St. Helena, French boundaries were further constricted, and an indemnity of 700,000,000 francs was levied upon the redoubtable and troublesome nation. But three years later, when it appeared that the Bourbon government was soundly entrenched, the armies of occupation withdrew, and France was permitted to join the four victor powers in a quintuple alliance.

Seven years after Waterloo the régime of Louis XVIII was offered a special chance to demonstrate its dependable conservatism. The Congress of Verona (with the British government dissenting) authorized Louis to send a French army into Spain to suppress liberal manifestations there and to buttress the shaken throne of that despicable Bourbon, Ferdinand VII. The pendulum of French foreign policy had travelled a full arc since the defiant day, thirty years earlier, when the First French Republic proclaimed a war against all kings. France was no longer 'the revolutionary nation', and the forbidden music of the *Marseillaise* seemed the fading echo of a fantastic dream. In 1821 Napoleon died on St. Helena. His son and heir, 'the Eaglet', raised in Vienna under Metternich's watchful eye, was the shadow of a great name, an unhappy youth destined to an early death. Legitimacy had triumphed, reaction was the order of the day, and Europe had apparently recovered from 'the poison of French ideas'.

Having vanquished Napoleon and re-established peace, the British, Russian, Austrian, and Prussian governments pledged themselves in 1815 to a twenty-year pact of friendship. Their spokesmen stressed their intention to preserve the peace settlement intact and to perpetuate the Concert of Europe through 'government by conferences'. At Aix-la-Chapelle (1818) the international machinery creaked, but it still functioned. But at the conference of Troppau and Laibach (1820–1) the British government was already at odds with its continental allies over the question of joint interference in the affairs of troubled nations. Metternich and his conservative colleagues were alarmed at the student agitation in German universities and the revolutionary outbreaks in Naples and Spain. Despite British dissent the governments of Austria, Prussia, and Russia endorsed the 'Troppau Protocol', declaring that any state that suffered a change of government through revolution would be excluded from the European Concert. When the three powers voted to intervene in Spain Britain declined to co-operate. George Canning, who had become British foreign secretary after Castlereagh's suicide (1822), withdrew England from the 'European Areopagus', and the Congress of Verona in that year marked the parting of the ways. Thus the Quadruple Alliance lost meaning before half its projected twenty years had passed, and the Tory government in London, hated by liberals at home, became the hope of liberals abroad.

This resumption by Great Britain of its traditional policy of isolation nullified the congress system. The exalted post-war mood of 1815 had evaporated already, and its most idealistic expression, the Holy Alliance proposed by Alexander I of Russia, was already dead. Alexander's messianic proposition to his colleagues, that 'the sole principle of force, whether between the said Governments or between their Subjects, shall be that of doing each other reciprocal service', had been accepted 'in principle' by most of his fellow princes, but it exerted no visible influence on their policies. By 1822 the remembered idealism and sacrifice of the war years had given way to the calculations and compromises of peace. Canning welcomed the return to a more realistic diplomacy of 'every nation for itself and God for us all', and Britain resumed an independent course in European and world affairs.

With this weakening of the European Concert the second factor listed earlier—the predominance of British sea power—became a decisive influence, especially when it operated against the conservative alliance. Within the heart of Europe the governments of Austria, Prussia, and Russia might work their will, but no state with a sea coast, or a sea trade, or overseas colonies could ignore the British maritime pressure. Ferdinand VII of Spain learned this promptly when Canning granted conditional recognition (1822) to the governments set up by the rebellious Spanish colonists in South America, where the valiant labours of Simon Bolivar, the Liberator, and José de San Martin had established independent republics from Caracas to Chile. The conservative powers sympathized with Ferdinand's 'legitimate' claim to Spanish America; the Russian government offered him ships to carry a punitive force to the New World; but British aid to the rebels and British control of the seas made such an expedition impracticable. Trade with the new republics was already yielding the English rich rewards, and enterprising London bankers had found promising fields for investment in Latin America. They had no wish to see Spain reassert a rigid economic monopoly over its lost empire of nearly four million square miles and twelve to fifteen million inhabitants.

European colonial exploitation of the New World was at an end, and it was a New World nation, fittingly enough, that proclaimed this fact to the European cabinets. In his annual message to the Congress of the United States in 1823, President James Monroe declared it to be 'a principle in which the rights and interests of the United States are involved, that the American continents, by the free and independent condition which they have assumed and maintain, are henceforth not to be considered as subjects for future colonization by any European powers'.

The immediate incentive for this historic announcement was a proposal from the Russian government to Britain and the United States suggesting that the three nations define their interests in the Pacific coast of North America. But a more urgent motive inspiring Monroe was the fear that Spain, with the backing of the European alliance, might regain control over the South American republics that had so recently declared their independence. The political system of the European monarchies, the President emphasized, was essentially different from that of the Americas. 'We owe it, therefore, to candour', he wrote, 'and to the amicable relations existing between the United States and those powers to declare that we should consider any attempt on their part to extend their system to any portion of this hemisphere as dangerous to our peace and safety.'

This bold rebuke to the allied sovereigns by a fledgling republic would not by itself have blocked their intentions. The Monroe Doctrine became a cornerstone of United States foreign policy because it was reinforced by the might of the British fleet. Canning had, in fact, proposed a joint Anglo-American declaration, but the statesmen at Washington distrusted the British intentions. As issued, Monroe's message took the form of an independent gesture, important chiefly because of its later amplifications. The United States Congress passed no legislation ratifying it at the time, and the European powers affected to treat it with disdain. But the fact remained that Great Britain and the United States had both indicated their common, though independent, intention to preserve the liberty of the Spanish American republics. As an immediate consequence Spain forfeited all chance of regaining the colonial revenues that had so long sustained its failing economy. But there was a second result of much greater and more permanent significance. The exclusion of European pressure and European armies from the New World meant that for a century the United States was to be spared the cost of maintaining a large military establishment to defend its frontiers. The light taxes and the large measure of individual freedom that Americans came to prize so highly were not wholly the result of their free republican institutions. Rather, the development of those institutions was dependent upon the absence of strong and militant neighbours, and upon the security derived from political and geographical isolation. *Amerika, du hast es besser*, Goethe observed with his usual prescience, and he predicted a time when the New World nations would rival the achievements of the Old, and their argosies would glean the trade of both oceans through the severed isthmus of Panama.

Their freedom secured, the American republics were persuaded at first that they wished to live to themselves. 'In the wars of European powers in matters relating to themselves we have never taken any part,' Monroe proclaimed, 'nor does it comport with our policy so to do.' But the severance of political bonds did not dissolve the cultural and economic ties that bound the Americas to Europe. By 1815 the United States had already waged several campaigns against the pirate fleets of Tripoli and Algiers in defence of its Mediterranean commerce; and ten years later the Mediterranean again captured American attention when the Greeks rose in rebellion against their Turkish masters. The creation of Philhellenic societies from Boston to Buenos Aires suggested that educated Americans had read Herodotus no less assiduously than their European cousins and were equally eager to identify the modern Greeks with the ancient Athenians and the Turks with the Persians. The cause of Greek independence made a powerful appeal to all men of classical training and of liberal impulses, a combination of sentiments certain to embarrass the conservative statesmen who were striving to hold Europe to a cult of immobility.

Metternich's first impulse was to let the Greek revolt

burn itself out 'beyond the pale of civilization'. The Turkish sultan, Mahmud II, asked nothing better, and left his commanders in the Morea a free hand to make a solitude and call it peace. But the prolonged resistance of the Greeks won admiration throughout Christendom, and by 1827 Britain, Russia, and France had combined to arbitrate the six-year-old struggle. When the Turks proved obdurate the naval forces of the three powers destroyed a Turco-Egyptian fleet in Navarino Bay, and in 1829 the treaty of Adrianople guaranteed the independence of Greece. The republic which the Greeks had proclaimed was subsequently transformed into a monarchy and a Bavarian prince crowned below the ruins of the Acropolis as Otto I, King of the Hellenes. Republics, it seemed, were still out of fashion. But a rebellion had been condoned, a government changed by violence, and a new national state created. Liberals took hope from this breach in the ramparts of conservatism, and the Greek revolt proved the opening tremor of a general political eruption. One year after the treaty of Adrianople all Europe was ablaze with the revolutionary outbreaks of 1830.

The signal for this new series of popular insurrections came, aptly enough, from Paris. Louis XVIII had maintained a working balance between liberal and reactionary forces under a constitutional charter, but he died in 1824, leaving the throne to his stiff-necked brother, Charles X. Within five years Charles perpetrated a succession of blunders that recalled the ill-starred reign of James II in England. He sought to reward the old French nobility at the expense of the rising bourgeoisie,

defied the Chambers by appointing reactionary ministers, and finally attempted a *coup d'état*, declaring the
press censored, the Chambers of Deputies dissolved,
and three-fourths of the electorate disfranchised. These
ordinances of 26 July 1830 were Charles's last official
edicts. Four days later Paris was in the control of an
insurgent mob, the tricolour waved from Notre-Dame,
and the king was in flight.

'Gentlemen, saddle your horses! France is in revolution again,' exclaimed Nicholas I when word of the July
days reached St. Petersburg. Metternich was less resolute. The news from Paris threw him into a mood of
unwonted depression, and as Frederick William III of
Prussia was as hesitant as ever the Troppau Protocol
remained a dead letter. More imminent threats soon
made joint intervention by the eastern powers a risky
venture in any case, for the July revolution set off a
chain reaction, igniting revolts in Belgium, Switzerland,
Italy, the Germanies, and Poland. The Austrian,
Russian, and Prussian governments could not afford to
move into western Europe, where the liberals won and
held important ground in the ferment of 1830–2. These
liberal gains will be traced in the following chapter:
they stretched out into the future. But in central and
eastern Europe the weight of the past proved too heavy
to lift, and the revolts of 1830 expired in bloodshed and
frustration. All the major forces there, political, military, economic, and geographic, prescribed this negative
outcome. After 1830 Europe was divided more positively
than before into a progressive and a reactionary camp,
into a western group of parliamentary governments and

an eastern league of authoritarian monarchies. The main source of liberal strength was a powerful bourgeoisie; where no aggressive middle class could seize the reins of government the liberal drive collapsed.

It was logical that Britain and France should be the first powers to break away from the unenlightened rigidity of the Restoration programme. Britain forsook the European alliance in 1822 over the Spanish question. France defied the conservative monarchies in 1830 by a change of dynasty. Both nations were economically progressive; both had discarded the semi-feudal institutions and outmoded social distinctions of earlier centuries; both sympathized with less advanced neighbours who were seeking political emancipation and responsible government. There was, in the first half of the nineteenth century, a profound ideological conflict dividing liberal from conservative Europe, a conflict induced and intensified by the irresistible expansion of new economic forces. The peoples of north-western Europe, with the British in the lead, had developed institutions of representative government. But in central and eastern Europe the older system of monarchical despotism still fought to maintain itself; and the disposal of the national revenue, the command of the army, the censorship of the press, and the liberties of the individual remained in the hands of ministers who were responsible not to the nation but to the Crown. In the reactionary states of Europe the people remained subjects, in the liberal states they had become citizens.

Where the sceptre passed from an absolute monarch to a sovereign people the executive power devolved upon

a ministerial cabinet responsible to a parliamentary
majority. This political transition was the outward and
visible sign of an economic and social revolution. It
meant that the class structure inherited from the Middle
Ages, the stratification of society into castes which set
the privileged groups of nobles and clergy in opposition
to the vast unprivileged majority, was yielding to an
alternative class structure founded on a more dynamic
economic system. The capitalist economy had created
three new classes, a capitalist minority whose power
and profits were derived primarily from investments,
a 'middle class' dependent in part upon property and
in part upon payment for services, and a proletarian
majority whose members had almost no resources in
land or savings and lived on wages. As the older privileged groups, the nobles and clergy, were supplanted
and dispossessed, control passed to a new emergent
aristocracy, the capitalists, who allied themselves with
the upper bourgeoisie to establish a form of government
that would safeguard their wealth and influence. The
liberal philosophy that was formulated to justify this
shift concealed an implicit contradiction, and involved
a denial of justice that discredited the bourgeois synthesis. For the liberal creed preached the equality of all
citizens before the law, but liberalism in practice too
often concealed, behind a façade of democratic reforms,
the concentration of the economic surplus in the hands
of a narrowing minority. To hostile critics the evolution
of the capitalist system appeared little better than the
substitution of industrial serfdom for agrarian serfdom, and they insisted that government under the new

régime remained what it had been under the old, 'the conspiracy of the few against the many'.

The rise of a capitalist economy in Europe may be seen as three consecutive phases of the same movement. The first period, from the close of the Middle Ages to the last years of the eighteenth century, was primarily an era of commercial capitalism. This was followed by an interval of about half a century during which industrial capitalism played a noteworthy part and many leading entrepreneurs increased their influence by investing their surplus wealth in the newly mechanized industries and in steam transportation. After 1850 the powerful role of the banks and financial agencies, which won a voice in business ventures through loans and the flotation of stocks, inaugurated the phase of finance capitalism that lasted into the twentieth century. It is obvious that no rigid dates can be assigned to mark the exact moment of transition from one phase to the next, but it is convenient to distinguish the forms that capitalist enterprise assumed in these successive periods.

The years from 1815 to 1830 fall within the period of industrial capitalism. As new inventions multiplied and the application of power revolutionized spinning and weaving, far-sighted factory owners made fortunes, and mushroom cities grew up around the mills. In seizing this golden opportunity British entrepreneurs enjoyed advantages that placed them half-a-century ahead of their continental competitors. The foreign export trade of Great Britain had trebled in the revolutionary period (1789–1815), and the profits were largely concentrated

c

in the hands of men with the vision and initiative to ride the waves of the future. Iron and coal for an industrial civilization were available in England at convenient centres. The Enclosure Acts (over two and a half million acres were enclosed between 1802 and 1844) created larger and more efficient agricultural estates, but drove thousands of cottagers and small landholders to seek work in the towns, thus providing an abundance of cheap labour. British mechanics equalled and probably surpassed those of the Continent, and British capital was available to finance the new factories. In addition, Britain commanded raw materials, markets, and transportation routes. A dominant navy, an extensive colonial empire, and a merchant marine larger than all others combined, assured a constant influx of supplies and the ready export of manufactures to distant buyers. Lastly, to crown this unique combination of colonial, commercial, industrial, maritime, and naval leadership, Britain assumed the leading role in international finance, and London supplanted Amsterdam as the banking centre of Europe. By 1815 the Bank of England was the largest centre of deposit in the world, and when it resumed specie payments in 1819 its notes were the only negotiable paper that circulated throughout Europe at their face value in gold.

British economic leadership after 1815 increased the difficulties under which other European business groups laboured. France should have been an enterprising and redoubtable rival for world markets. But French commerce had been crippled by the long years of sea blockade, and did not recover until 1825 the volume of foreign trade it had enjoyed in 1789. French industry, free to exploit the European markets while Napoleon's power endured, suffered a sharp set-back with his fall, and could not compete favourably with the flood of British manufactures when peace unsealed the continental ports. French capital remained timid, French smelters still used wood, though coal was available, French manufacturers were satisfied with local customers when national markets alone could justify the installations and the investment required for large-scale production. The Revolution had cleared the ground, emancipated the bourgeoisie, abolished internal tariffs and bureaucratic obstructions. Yet France, a country of 200,000 square miles and 30,000,000 people (twice the area and population of Great Britain), could not meet the competition of English textiles or Russian wheat. French farmers and industrialists clamoured for more protection in order to hold their local markets, and then failed to meet even these limited demands. Lack of capital undoubtedly delayed the rise of large-scale industry in France. But a more alert and responsive government in Paris might have encouraged investors by limiting their liability and easing the law of bankruptcy, or have provided loans or subsidies to equip more efficient foundries and larger factories. In Belgium, where statesmen of greater vision directed the economic programme, the mechanization of industry made swifter progress, especially after the Belgians revolted against their forced union with the Dutch in 1830. While the French were still apathetic, Belgium led all Europe in railway construction, and the first lines were state enterprises, intelligently planned to stimulate trade and promote industry.

East of the Rhine the embryo industries produced by the age of steam faced the additional handicap of political separatism. For the Germanies still were divided into some thirty-eight fragments, and there could be no national market while this particularism endured. The advantages that would follow the adoption of a uniform currency, a uniform tariff policy, a uniform system of commercial law and weights and measures, predisposed the German business groups to favour political consolidation. When the reactionary settlement of 1815 postponed this hope indefinitely, the Prussian government took the lead in broadening the economic foundations for nationhood, despite opposition from Vienna and from some south German states. In 1818 all manufactured goods entering any of the scattered Hohenzollern domains were subjected to a moderate 10 per cent. *ad valorem* duty, while a heavy transit charge was imposed on merchandise passing *through* Prussian controlled areas. This economic pressure helped to persuade the governments of several adjoining German states that it would be advisable to enter the customs union. Within a generation the Zollverein included the greater part of north Germany, making the area a free internal market in which fiscal uniformity prevailed. All products entering this area were subject to the common tariff, the proceeds of which were distributed to the member states of the Zollverein in proportion to their population.

Outside the countries named—Britain, France,

Belgium, the Germanies—the coming industrial trans-formation had carved few scars on the European landscape by 1830. Transportation and communication were still slow and costly, limited by the capacity of the stage-coach, the river barge, and the sailing ship. Four-fifths of the European people lived parochial lives in rural surroundings. Towns had outgrown their ancient walls but not their quaint, half-medieval aspect. City skylines were still dominated by the church spires, visible leagues away in clear weather, 'all bright and glittering in the smokeless air'. Even in England, where industrialism was most advanced, the pall of factory smoke had not yet spread its darkening canopy, and the urbanization of society, that was to turn four English-men out of five into town dwellers within a century, still lay in the future.

How little the nascent energies of the industrial age influenced the thought and culture of the time is apparent from its literature and art. The poets and philosophers who influenced European thought most powerfully after 1815 were critical, as always, of the society of their day, but when they projected a better world they prophesied the shape of things to come almost exclusively in terms of their own bookish precon-ceptions. Few thinkers showed any genuine interest or deep understanding for the current economic trends, the new forces that were changing European culture, predominantly agrarian since its immemorial origins, into an industrial civilization such as the world had never seen.

Major intellectual currents in the Restoration era

were confused by petulant whirls and eddies and the
prevailing mood was one of widespread disillusionment.
Temporarily, it seemed as if all the glittering generalities
of the eighteenth century were tarnished. The rationalist
quest for a perfect, workable ground-plan for society
had miscarried. The revolutionary dreamers who had
clutched at a syllogistic paradise for a regenerated
humanity were discredited. As the vision splendid faded
into the light of common day, Wordsworth composed a
nostalgic dirge for the bright, misleading dawn of 1789,

> In which the meagre, stale, forbidding ways
> Of custom, law, and statute took at once
> The attraction of a country in romance.

Like most of his generation, Wordsworth had been
sobered by experience, and he accepted the Restoration
settlement as a necessary compromise, a sensible *mariage
de convenance* contracted above the grave of a dream.
Shelley might still insist with rapt defiance that poets
were 'the unacknowledged legislators of the world', but
by 1815 they were legislators without a mandate. The
peoples of Europe had to learn anew to put their trust
in princes and in the prosaic administrators the princes
approved. Reformers with a blueprint for Utopia found
no patrons at the Restoration courts. 'To the dreamers',
Metternich recorded with pompous superfluity, 'I have
never belonged.'

An incurable distrust of journalists, especially of
writers with adventurous ideas, infected the official
circles of Restoration society. Monarchs no longer
honoured knights of the pen who attacked social abuses,
as Frederick the Great and Catherine of Russia had

once honoured Voltaire and Diderot. On the contrary, outspoken critics of State and Church after 1815 found themselves in difficulties with the censors and the secret police, and liberal professors were driven from their chairs in the universities. Even in England the 'panic of the French Revolution' inspired the Six Acts of 1819, which restricted public gatherings, authorized the seizure of seditious or blasphemous articles, and subjected pamphlets to a heavy stamp duty. In the outcome such attempts to control the press and to silence criticism had little measurable effect, but they undoubtedly intensified the febrile and frustrated mood of many European intellectuals in this winter of their discontent.

The spirit of Romanticism, already quickening European literature and art in the last quarter of the eighteenth century, reached its apogee in the decades after 1815. No check imposed upon political insurgence could halt the Romantic revolt; on the contrary it seemed as if ardent souls, denied the opportunity to act their dreams, applied themselves the more intensely to dream their actions. Romanticism was a coat of many colours; it matched the uniform of no one political party; but it met the needs of a generation shaken from its conventional certainties by the impact of prodigious events. Great collective efforts like the French Revolution leave a vacuum in their wake. The European imagination, wearied by contemporary realities, sought escape in the idealized historical novels of Walter Scott, in the dramas of Schiller, in the lyrics, ballads, and romances of fantasy-haunted writers, from Coleridge to

Manzoni and from Herder to Heine, who saw a light that never was on land or sea. It is customary to speak of the Romantic movement as a revolt against the sterile truths of science and the rigidity of classical formulas, and the dictum is true in that Romanticism spoke the language of the heart and repudiated artificial patterns in favour of 'unpremeditated art'. Historically, however, it is more important to note that although the aspirations of the Romantic writers often triumphed over logic and reason they triumphed over little else. The heroes of Romantic tragedy, like their poetic creators, sought a life beyond life and a love beyond love, and they found themselves condemned to a common fate: frustration. When an entire generation takes such frustrated heroes to its heart, the historian is forced to seek the answer in social conditions rather than in aesthetic aims.

Georg Brandes, the Danish literary critic, related this mood of defeat, of abdication, to the effects of the French Revolution, suggesting that the removal of social barriers left ambitious and impressionable youths without an adequate excuse for failure in their quest for fame. In revenge, they found a scornful solace in repudiating the unappreciative world they could not conquer. Such an explanation is inviting, but it does not go deep enough. The generation that survived the French Revolution had watched a supreme assault of the human spirit break itself upon the ramparts of social inequality. All classes agreed by 1815 (though for divergent reasons) that the Revolution had been a failure, and such universal disillusionment craved its sublimation. The flame of revolt still burned secretly, 'like a lamp in a tomb', knitting a million readers in a vicarious kinship with those superb and tragic rebels, from Faust to Manfred, who defied destiny and scorned the world's incomprehension. The true altar of the Romantic poets was not the temple of the muses; it was an icy peak in the Caucasus, and their god was a tormented Titan. The Romanticism of the Restoration era was a Promethean cult.

Like most protest movements, the Romantic revolt was stronger in emotion than in logic and it produced singularly few works distinguished by structural integration and completeness. No new philosophy emerged in these years to justify the political settlement. The most influential thinker of the age, Georg Wilhelm Friedrich Hegel, evolved a synthesis of ideas that served both radicals and reactionaries as an arsenal of arguments. All political groups were equally impelled by the urge to find a satisfactory principle of authority, but it was a quest in which none succeeded. In England, liberal intellectuals digested the chill utilitarianism of Jeremy Bentham. In France some rationalists still attempted to found a secular society on a universal substructure of natural law, but they were in discredit. Scant attention greeted Auguste Comte's *Plan of the Scientific Operations necessary for the Reorganization of Society* (1822), and this early approach to the problem of scientific sociology had to await a climate of opinion more favourable to its acceptance. Across the Rhine, Friedrich Karl von Savigny indicted the French Civil Code as narrow and mechanical, and denounced the effort to extract social postulates from natural law in his essay *On the Vocation of our Age for Legislation and Jurisprudence* (1814). But Savigny offered no satisfactory alternative, for he concluded that the time was not yet ripe for a system of legislation based on a sound philosophic study of historical development.

In this general search for a principle of authority that would justify governments in exercising sovereign power the champions of the Restoration Settlement proved no more successful than their antagonists. If neither natural law as revealed by science and reason nor historical tradition embalmed in ancient statutes could provide an acceptable basis for social control, there remained only the older concept of divine law expressed in the Scriptures and in the dogmas of the Roman Catholic Church. This theocratic foundation had buttressed the canon and civil law of earlier centuries and was still available for those who would put their faith in it. Joseph de Maistre reformulated the Catholic traditionalist position in successive works culminating in *Du pape* (1819), but as he made papal supremacy the central doctrine of his system neither Protestant nor Catholic monarchs were willing to endorse an argument that subordinated their authority to that of the Pope. At the other extreme in the range of Catholic political speculation stood Félicité Robert de Lamennais, who denounced the rationalists for their adoration of science as the source of all truth and progress, and sought to revivify religion by urging liberal reforms within the Church. His anomalous blend of ultramontane tenets with pleas for free speech and a free press embroiled him with his fellow clericals in France, and in 1831 he carried his appeal to Rome. Pope Gregory XVI condemned his teaching, and Lamennais, defying the papal censure, thenceforth carried on his reforming efforts outside the Church.

A religious revival, a genuine spiritual quickening, touched all parts of Europe in these early decades of the nineteenth century, but the organized churches resisted rather than inspired it. Much of its strength was a carry-over from the humanitarian idealism of the revolutionary era, for humanitarianism was the only tenet of the revolutionary cult that survived undiscredited and undiminished. The Methodists in England, the Pietists in the Germanies, and the Society of Friends (Quakers) wherever they lived and worked, insisted on the need to improve social conditions, reform the jails and asylums, mitigate the penal laws, and abolish slavery and the slave trade. Anti-slavery agitation in Great Britain, which culminated in its abolition throughout the empire owed much to the Christian zeal of the evangelical sects. Quakers and Methodists devoted themselves to many of the humanitarian aims that the legislation of the French Revolution had championed, but their humane programme was not an endorsement of the Revolution itself. On the contrary, the growth of the Nonconformist congregations, in England for example (where they came to include almost half the population), helped to inoculate the nation against revolutionary ideas. The rationalist assault had been delivered against institutions; the religious revival appealed to the conscience, and the popular preachers sought to regenerate society by converting the individuals who composed it. Where the Revolution had emphasized the rights of the citizen as the foundation of a just society, the religious revival stressed the duties of the Christian as the clue to the good life.

In their ultimate aims both the rationalists and the leaders of the religious revival were seeking a greater measure of social justice. Advocates of democracy saw it as the foreordained solution, arguing that when all citizens received the franchise governments would become truly popular because they would be truly representative. Across the Atlantic the principle that governments derive their just powers from the consent of the governed had already been firmly established by 1815, and democracy suffered no temporary set-back as in Europe. The faith that all adult (male) citizens should have a voice in choosing their legislators was vindicated in regular elections, and the rapid growth of population in the United States, from 8,000,000 in 1815 to 12,000,000 in 1830, demonstrated the practicality of popular republican institutions. The year 1828 brought the boisterous election of Andrew Jackson as seventh president, a notable triumph for the popular party that placed in the White House a son of the frontier whose heart was with the common people. In France the middle classes were gathering their forces for the overthrow of Charles X, and in England the period of Tory Administration was drawing to a close. Repeal of the Test and Corporation Acts (1828) and the passage of the Roman Catholic Emancipation Act (1829) removed the civil restrictions and disabilities under which dissident religious groups had laboured. Throughout western Europe the forces of democracy were resuming their interrupted march, and the results were shortly to appear in the liberal victories of 1830–2.

Empire

1815

Chapter Two

LIBERAL GAINS AND ROMANTIC FRUSTRATIONS (1830-48)

THE French were no longer *la grande nation* after Waterloo; they were a defeated people saddled with an unpopular monarchy and sufficiently chastened to make the best of it. Every class and group, however, had a grievance. The old nobility and the higher clergy mourned their lost privileges. The middle classes distrusted the restored Bourbon dynasty and sought to hold and extend the legal and political gains the Revolution had brought them. A growing city proletariat demanded recognition and better living conditions. Chauvinists dreamed of a military revival that would regild the imperial eagles. The fact that these divided factions were held for fifteen years in a precarious balance did not augur that the old and the new France could be reconciled; it merely proved that momentarily the desire for order and stability overrode all other impulses. Throughout the Restoration period the Right and the Left, the Ultras and the Radicals, remained locked in opposition, manœuvring for advantage under a truce that neither accepted as permanent, while a group of moderates in the centre kept the system working. It was not a glorious period nor a memorable one, but it enabled the French people to recover from the

exhaustion of war and to test the advan
limited, constitutional monarchy.

Charles X upset this restoration comprom
refusal to play the limited role of a cons   unal
monarch. From his accession in 1824 he leaned steadily
towards the Right, and when opposition mounted he
attempted to distract the nation by dispatching a
punitive expedition to seize Algiers (July 1830). This
renewal of colonial expansion laid the cornerstone for
later French empire in Africa, but at the time it failed
to improve Charles's position or to appease the Parisians.
Election returns presented the king with a defiant
chamber that once again demanded the resignation of
the unpopular Polignac ministry. Instead of yielding,
Charles resorted to government by ordinance, dissolving the chamber, abridging the franchise, suspending
the liberty of the press, and decreeing a new election.
This violation of the charter (as the liberals understood
it) provoked the Parisian populace to an immediate
insurrection which the king had failed to provide against
and within three days he was in flight. The fate of
another Bourbon had been settled on the barricades of
Paris before the people of France could be consulted
or even informed of the event.

It is significant that in this July crisis of 1830 the
moderates counted until the last moment on a parliamentary victory to give them control of the ministry.
They had no real wish for a revolution or a reversion to
the discredited expedient of a republic, which was still
associated with the Jacobin dictatorship. Swiftly rallying their forces, they nominated Louis Philippe of

D

Orleans, head of a collateral branch of the royal house, to the vacant throne. These bourgeois politicians, who represented the propertied classes, dreaded the demands of an armed and victorious proletariat more than they feared the designs of a despotic king, and they manœuvred themselves adroitly into power between the opposing dangers. The middle classes welcomed Louis Philippe as a 'citizen king' who would reign but not govern, and they were determined to control the new régime by preserving their majority in the chamber of deputies.

In its outcome, the French Revolution of 1830 was less a revolution than a reaffirmation of the Charter of 1814. The charter was re-edited to eliminate ambiguous clauses and to redefine the French government as a limited monarchy, constitutional, representative, and responsible. The right to vote, though extended to 250,000 electors instead of 100,000, remained the prerogative of 'men of property', and this oligarchic group who possessed the franchise (numerically a mere one per cent. of the nation) spoke for France in terms of their own class interests. To placate the more radical elements of the populace the tricolour flag of the Revolution was substituted once again for the white flag of the Bourbon monarchy, and the ban on the singing of the Marseillaise was rescinded. At the same time, however, Louis Philippe made it clear that the July Monarchy would launch no revolutionary crusade against neighbouring states as the First French Republic had done. Reassured on this point, the European courts decided to recognize the new 'King of the

French', and even Nicholas I of Russia addressed him as *Sire* although he declined to employ the more customary diplomatic greeting of *mon bon frère*.

The cautious foreign policy of the July Monarchy disappointed French republicans and chauvinists. Italian, German, and Polish revolutionaries who organized revolts in the hope of French support were likewise disillusioned. Outbreaks in Parma, Modena, and Rome were suppressed by Austrian troops. Agitation in the Germanies frightened a few princes into concessions, but firm counter-pressure by the Austrian and Prussian governments checked the liberal movement throughout central Europe, and by 1833 Metternich could congratulate himself that his system was 'triumphantly fireproof'. The Polish insurrection burned more fiercely, until internal divisions and lack of foreign aid doomed it, leaving Tsar Nicholas free to treat Russian Poland as a conquered country subject to martial law.

In Switzerland, the Iberian states, and Belgium, the reactionary powers could not intervene without risking war with France or Britain, and there the liberal groups improved their position. Most of the Swiss cantons established new constitutions by 1833, proclaiming the sovereignty of the people, the liberty of the press, and the equality of all citizens before the law. In Spain and Portugal disputes arose over the royal succession. England and France supported the Spanish regent, Maria Cristina, against her brother-in-law, Don Carlos, and the latter was sent into exile. Don Miguel, pretender to the Portuguese throne, shared the same fate after French and British pressure had set his niece, Maria II, on the throne in Lisbon. Both Iberian states were to be rent for years by civil strife, but liberals in general regarded the settlements reached there between 1830 and 1834 as victories for the western, constitutional powers. The reactionary governments of Austria, Prussia, and Russia, which favoured Don Carlos and Don Miguel, recalled their representatives from Madrid while France and Britain entered into a 'quadruple alliance' with Spain and Portugal to preserve constitutional reforms.

The case of Belgium provided an even clearer test o strength between the absolutist (eastern) and constitutional (western) bloc. Unhappy in their forced alliance with the Dutch, decreed by the Congress of Vienna, the Belgian liberals rose in rebellion when they learned that the Parisians had dethroned Charles X. William I of the United Netherlands was extremely reluctant to lose half his kingdom, but the absolutist governments failed to aid him with military forces while the western powers supported the Belgian secessionists, and these circumstances decided the issue. Belgium was established as an independent state, and Leopold of Saxe-Coburg (a German prince who had become a British citizen) accepted the throne and married the daughter of Louis Philippe. This settlement was a tacit recognition that the fate of Belgium depended primarily on the attitude of France and Britain. At London the ambassadors of the five great powers (Britain, France, Austria, Prussia, and Russia) acknowledged the independence of Belgium and guaranteed its perpetual neutrality. The new state took its place among the nations as a constitutional monarchy under a charter that proclaimed the sovereignty of the nation, the supremacy of the legislative over the executive power, and the extension of the franchise on a broader base than the English or the French people enjoyed in 1830. The right to vote was still limited to a minority of the Belgian citizens with the requisite property qualifications, but there could be no question that the forces of liberalism had gained one more victory. Nor could there be any doubt that the British fleet (which blockaded Dutch ports until William I yielded) and the French military forces (which expelled the Dutch from Belgian territories) had made the independence of Belgium possible.

The electoral reforms introduced in France and Belgium in 1830–1 were sober compromises; no group except the extreme radicals had seriously proposed that the ballot should be granted to all adult citizens. Yet the fact that the franchise could be broadened at all without precipitating a social revolution made 1830 a turning-point in nineteenth-century history. For two generations the governing classes of Europe had been haunted by the memory of 1789, and fear that the smallest concession to popular demands would prove an invitation to chaos made conservative statesmen and churchmen uncompromising opponents of political change. Even in England, where the need to reform the electoral system had been emphasized by the younger Pitt in 1785, the 'panic of the French Revolution' postponed the project for nearly fifty years. After 1830 it could be postponed no longer.

Two major groups were working to reform the British parliamentary system when the news of the July revolution in France arrived to quicken their hopes. Whig leaders wanted a redistribution of seats in the House of Commons, for the shift of population from the south-east to the industrial north-west meant that a number of declining and half-depopulated boroughs still sent members of Parliament while large cities of recent growth, such as Liverpool and Manchester, lacked representation. The spokesmen who championed the working classes had more radical demands. They wanted an extension of the suffrage that would give a vote to the factory hands and the farm labourers, thus enabling them to elect their own delegates to Westminster to secure remedial legislation. When these two groups joined forces the long rule of the Tory party came to an end, and in 1831 the Whigs won a clear majority in the House of Commons for the first time in half a century. The electors had voted for reform, but the House of Lords refused once again to pass the bill sent up from the Commons. Rioting spread dangerously and the deadlock was not broken until the Whig leader, Lord Grey, obtained an assurance from William IV that he would appoint sufficient new peers to outvote the opposition in the House of Lords. The threat sufficed, and in June 1832 enough recalcitrant Tory nobles and bishops abstained from voting to permit the Bill to pass the upper house.

The Reform Bill of 1832 reflected the divided aims of the groups that had secured its passage. Fifty-six boroughs that had previously returned 111 members were disfranchised, and thirty-two others lost one member each. The seats thus made available were redistributed, twenty-two large towns acquiring two each, twenty-one towns receiving one apeice, while the county membership was almost doubled. Separate bills were adopted to remodel the franchise on similar lines in Scotland and Ireland, but the measures did not establish equal electoral districts or anticipate future shifts in population. Though Lord Grey insisted that the Bill was 'final' it was in reality a moderate compromise that bitterly disappointed the radical leaders who had backed the Whigs in the expectation of far-reaching reforms. The franchise remained the privilege of the few, for it was limited to householders paying ten pounds annual rental, with freeholders, copyholders, and leaseholders likewise subject to a ten-pound qualification. The actual increase in the number of voters throughout the British Isles was not great; the Reform Bill extended the franchise to some 813,000 voters where less than 500,000 had possessed it previously. Political power still rested in the hands of the wealthier classes, and the real significance of the new dispensation was that it shifted control from the agricultural and commercial aristocracy that had monopolized it since 1689 to the newer industrial aristocracy and the upper bourgeoisie. England remained an oligarchy after 1832, but an oligarchy in which the economic interests of the manufacturers had come to outweigh the agrarian interests of the landed class.

Proof that the centre of political power had shifted and that a new balance had been achieved could be read in the legislation passed by the 'reformed' parliament. The victorious Whigs emerged as the 'Liberal party' and the Tories came to be known as 'Conservatives'. An attempt by the king, William IV, to appoint a Tory prime minister in defiance of the Whig majority (1834) was promptly rebuked on appeal to the electors, and the principle was finally established that no cabinet could remain in power if it lost the confidence of a majority in the popular chamber. The accession of Victoria in 1837 opened the longest and most glorious reign in British annals, and the young queen was tutored in the responsibilities of a constitutional monarch by the Liberal prime minister, Lord Melbourne. Despite occasional friction, the new balance of political forces worked effectively and became famous as the Victorian Compromise. The two-party system remained the rule with Liberal and Conservative cabinets alternating at irregular intervals but dividing almost equally the sixty-four years of Victoria's reign.

In 1835 the Whigs consolidated their victory by the Municipal Corporations Act, which enabled the same urban electorate that had secured the parliamentary franchise three years earlier to dominate the local administration in the industrial cities. A more definitive test of the political and economic ascendency of the manufacturing interests came in 1846. Great Britain was moving steadily towards free trade, and import duties on many raw products and even on manufactured goods had been reduced or abandoned in deference to the demands of the business classes. But the country landowners, who formed the strongest group in the Tory party, clung to the import tariff on grains which enabled them to market their crops without undue fear of foreign competition. The Anti-Corn Law League, led by Richard Cobden and John Bright, assailed the Corn Laws as unjust on the ground that they kept the price of bread high for the benefit of the landowners at the expense of the urban consumers. When the Tory leader, Sir Robert Peel (who had headed the Conservative ministry since 1841), introduced a bill to establish free trade in grain he split the Tory party. But the Whigs supported the measure and the Corn Laws were repealed (1846). Free trade had won, and the repeal of the Navigation Acts three years later was a logical corollary. As the leading industrial nation in a world where agriculture was still a dominant form of economy, the British could maintain a more lucrative balance of trade and sell more manufactured wares if they accepted food and raw materials in exchange without hindrance. For Britian, therefore, the abandonment of import and export duties was a logical and profitable step. It was less easy to convince other peoples, especially nations with a nascent industrial economy, that they would gain by the same policy. 'Free trade', the aphoristic Disraeli observed pointedly in 1843, 'is not a principle, it is an expedient.'

Many British employers had supported repeal because it meant cheaper bread for their workers. Toward other social measures, that might war with their profits, they showed less enthusiasm. An inadequate bill to shorten the hours of labour in textile factories was passed in 1833. Labour conditions in mills and mines were often appalling, but it was a Tory ministry that introduced further reforms, sponsoring a mines act in 1842 and further factory legislation in 1844. The humanitarian impulses of the age often took odd and contradictory forms, as exemplified by the abolition of slavery in 1833 with compensation of £20,000,000 to colonial slave owners, while a simultaneous bill provided a modest £20,000 annually for public education in Britain. Reform of the poor-laws (1834) reflected the conflict between economic and philanthropic motives even more clearly, for it established such a harsh régime in the workhouses that it made pauperism appear a crime. Such, indeed, it seemed to many employers, who lacked workers and considered that all indigent persons capable of work should be persuaded to seek it by convincing them that they would find conditions in the workhouses worse than in the factories.

When the British labouring classes saw that the Reform Bill of 1832 failed to increase their representation or influence—that it had on the contrary entrenched their employers more firmly in power—they renewed their agitation. Some turned to direct bargaining, and as the Combination Laws that restricted worker's unions had been repealed in 1825, a Grand National Consolidated Trades Union took rapid form and claimed 500,000 members by 1834. The alarmed government struck back sharply, organizers received severe prison sentences, and the union collapsed. Popular leaders then reverted to political reform, and by 1838 they had drafted a 'People's Charter' which the radicals united in presenting to Parliament. The famous Six Points of

Chartism seem innocuous enough today, but in the 1830's and 1840's they were too extreme to please a legislature dominated by the propertied classes. The Chartists demanded universal manhood suffrage, secret ballot, annual elections, equal electoral districts, salaries for members of Parliament, and the abolition of property qualifications for those who stood for election. Despite widespread support the Chartists won no substantial concessions. Their final rally, in the stormy days of 1848, so frightened the authorities that the government appointed 170,000 special police to check the demonstrations. But the Chartist agitation had more sound than fury, and when the last monster petition was rejected by Parliament the movement collapsed.

Chartism was less an organized political drive than a protest movement the vigour of which fluctuated with economic conditions. British prosperity and business expansion between 1820 and 1848 was so remarkable that few malcontents could seriously challenge the advantages that accrued to the nation under middle-class rule. By 1840 Great Britain conducted 32 per cent. of the international trade of the world, more than three times as much as France which ranked second with 10 per cent. Had the British working classes been stirred by powerful revolutionary sentiments they would have rebelled after 1845, when poor harvests caused widespread wretchedness throughout Europe. The country most direfully affected by the famine of 1845–6 was Ireland, where the potato crop failed disastrously. Thousands starved and more thousands emigrated

from that most distressful country. Between 1740 and
1840 the population of Ireland had quadrupled, rising
from 2,000,000 to 8,000,000, thanks in part to the introduction of the potato. In the seventy years after 1845
the population fell almost 50 per cent. to 4,334,000 in
1914. No other European country suffered such a
catastrophic decline, and the falling birth-rate and mass
emigration that half-depopulated Ireland in the later
nineteenth century is the most telling indictment that
can be urged against British rule in the island that had
served as the earliest testing-ground for British conquest and colonization and proved the least successful.

While the French and British experimented with
electoral reform and a wider franchise after 1830, the
statesmen of eastern Europe looked on with doubt and
disapproval. A little democracy seemed a dangerous
thing to the sober bureaucrats of Vienna, Berlin, and
St. Petersburg, and they were not surprised to see the
workers of Paris and London riot for further concessions.
'The mob is now rising against the bourgeoisie',
Metternich remarked with the melancholy satisfaction
of one who has seen his warnings rejected and then
vindicated. A government that followed the shifting
moods of an unpredictable electorate could not, in his
opinion, maintain a consistent policy in domestic or
foreign affairs. He noted without surprise that the
Anglo-French accord of the early 1830's soon deterio-
rated and the two constitutional monarchies had drifted
close to war by 1840 because their interests clashed in
the eastern Mediterranean. Six years later a new Anglo-
French crisis arose when Louis Philippe betrothed his

youngest son, Anthony, to the Infanta Maria Louisa of Spain. The British foreign secretary, Lord Palmerston, appealed to Vienna for support, on the ground that a union of the French and Spanish dynasties would violate the treaty of Utrecht of 1713. Meternich replied sauvely that Austria had never recognized the more recent settlement by which the Spanish throne had passed to Isabella II instead of the male heir, Don Carlos. It amused him to see two parliamentary powers at odds over the anachronistic issue of a dynastic marriage, and he did nothing to heal their estrangement. Palmerston, however, was a dangerous man to bait. Piqued at Metternich, he retaliated by encouraging the Italian liberals, who hoped to drive the Austrians from northern Italy. Such trifling was highly dangerous to peace when the fires of nationalist and republican insurrection smouldered throughout Europe. By 1847 Metternich found himself on the defensive, while the British cabinet opened negotiations with the newly elected Pope, Pius IX, whose Italian sympathies and zeal for reforms aroused the deepest concern at Vienna. A *rapprochment* between the British government and the Vatican, if sincere, was a portent singular enough to startle the absolutist monarchs.

An unreasoning fear of all political innovations dominated the conservative courts. To outward view the solid front presented by Austria, Prussia, and Russia in the 1830's and 1840's made these three powers appear a triangular fortress, serene and steadfast in a disordered world. But internal weaknesses and the expanding roots of a new economic system were cracking their

rigid institutions. In Vienna the death of Francis I in
1835 bequeathed the Austrian throne to the incompe-
tent Ferdinand I, and the real power passed to a council
in which Metternich and Kolowrat were the most
active members. No efficient administration existed in
the Habsburg empire; there was no ministry, only
ministers; and subordinate functionaries remained
shackled by antiquated routines and their own invin-
cible indolence. Austrian society possessed notable
charms and virtues, a spirit of paternal benevolence
and filial piety, a tradition of leisure and gaiety and
good manners. There was a quaint affectionate devotion
to the Habsburg family, there was a cultured and elegant
aristocracy with a sense of *noblesse oblige*, there was a
heritage of lavish art and lilting music that formed a
unique contribution to the pattern of European culture.
But the historic statesmanship that had built an empire
on a foundation of fortunate marriages forsook the
Habsburg counsels in the nineteenth century, and the
divergent national aspirations of Germans, Magyars,
Slavs, and Italians undermined the imperial structure.
No common mood of patriotism appeared (as in
neighbouring empires) to create an Austrian nation, and
the half-autonomous kingdoms, duchies, and counties
seemed as loosely knit as oriental satrapies when com-
pared to the unified and centralized government of
nineteenth-century France. Even Metternich had been
known to admit that 'Asia begins on the Landstrasse'.

Few organs existed in the Habsburg lands through
which zeal for reform or popular dissatisfaction could
legitimately express itself. The provincial estates re-

presented the privileged groups; jealous of their pretensions the members resented advice from Vienna, and resisted appeals from below. Endless instructions were drafted and pigeon-holed—on the need for fiscal reforms, on the condition of the peasants, on the tariffs that stifled trade, on the discontent of the workers in the rising factories of Bohemia. In Hungry, where a few hundred magnates ruled with feudal complacency, the diet debated and deferred the projects of Stephen Szechenyi for legal and economic changes, for railroads to the west and steamboats on the Danube. The more radical demands of Louis Kossuth, who challenged the higher nobility, advocating a free press and a more representative parliament, brought him three years' imprisonment (1837–40). An awakening spirit of nationalism, intensified by the spread of Romanticism with its glorification of the historic past, quickened the desire for complete autonomy. Magyar superseded Latin as the official language in the diet, and literate Hungarians repudiated German to cultivate the beauties of their native tongue. These were the decades when German philologists prepared dictionaries on the popular dialects of Europe, making pedantry the servant of minority movements and history the handmaiden of national revolts. The Hungarian renascence and the Slavonic revival fed upon the folklore of the people, renovated by the scholars and romanticized by the writers. Literary circles became the focal centres of popular discontent, but the reforms debated there with passionate impracticability were too often intellectual extravaganzas void of substance. Meanwhile, the bureaucratic fortress at Vienna stood proudly aloof in its majestic inertia, the dust on its parchment folios unstirred by the winds of doctrine blowing through the salons.

In Berlin the governing officials displayed more competence and energy, for they had been trained under that famous Prussian system which the great Frederick had made a model of efficiency for the chancelleries of Europe. Unfortunately, the Hohenzollern bureaucracy was vulnerable at the apex: to function at its best it needed a monarch with administrative genius. Two centuries earlier the year 1640 had opened the patient constructive rule of the Great Elector; in 1740, Frederick the Great had commenced his brilliant and historic reign; but in 1840 a Hohenzollern prince with courage and tenacity was lacking. When the timid and reactionary Frederick William III died in that year, the crown passed to a Romantic mystic, Frederick William IV, whose unstable moods were to end in chronic insanity.

At the outset of his reign Frederick William IV raised unfounded hopes of reform among his more liberal and patriotic subjects. He charmed those about him with seductive promises and then disappointed them with repeated postponements. Behind his pose of pseudo-liberalism, his humane religiosity, lay a deep ancestral distrust of popular movements and parliamentary rule. His secret ideal of government was a despotism founded on persuasion; he released political prisoners and then denounced them because they failed to recant, relaxed the censorship and then restored it because the journalists criticized him. Destiny had prepared a leading role for Prussia in the drama of German unification, but Frederick William IV hesitated to march with the times, and the military strength and economic ascendency of the Prussian realm made it certain that German union could not advance if Prussia held back. Frequent admonitions from Vienna and St. Petersburg increased Frederick's irresolution but in 1847 he suddenly startled his admirers and his critics by convoking the provincial estates of the Hohenzollern domains to meet as a United Landtag. Liberal and national hopes ran high; but at the opening session the erratic monarch announced that his royal prerogatives must remain intact and that he would never permit the delegates to arrogate to themselves the authority of representatives of the people. This contradictory attitude typified the dilemma of the German nation. Historically and geographically the Germans stood between two worlds, the despotism of the past and the democracy of the future, the autocracy of Russian Tsardom and the bourgeois constitutionalism of Britain, France, and Belgium.

In St. Petersburg Nicholas I, Tsar and autocrat of all the Russias (1825–55), was plagued by no such inward conflicts. The mood of his reign was set in its opening year when he crushed the ill-fated Decembrist revolt inspired by a handful of liberal-minded army officers. The Polish uprising of 1830–1 hardened him in his conviction that any tampering with autocracy was a bid for rebellion, and he abrogated the constitution that Alexander I had granted to Russian Poland in 1815.

E

Nicholas had a barrack-room mentality, but he was not a blind reactionary nor an insensate martinet like his grandfather Paul I. He exercised his responsibilities in the mood of a conscientious disciplinarian. To ensure order he created the famous or infamous 'Third Section' of the imperial chancery, a special division of secret police organized to combat agitation and ferret out conspirators. Where legal and financial reforms promised greater efficiency he favoured them; the fiscal system was reorganized and a new code of Russian law promulgated in 1832. Criticism was curbed and liberal discussion silenced, even in the universities, but this censorship was relaxed in the sphere of technical education which made some notable advances. Mechanics and engineers were imported from western Europe, and the first Russian railway was opened in 1838. But the department of government always closest to the Tsar's heart was the army. It was the major bulwark of that 'Nicholas system' which, under the consecrated formula of Orthodoxy, Autocracy, and Nationalism, defended Holy Russia from attack and from the contamination of 'western ideas'.

No influential middle class of the western European type existed in Russia, no mercantile or industrial oligarchy wealthy and powerful enough to fight for constitutional reforms and a representative assembly with a responsible ministry. But the tides of the age had definitely turned against the old formulas of monarchical absolutism; it was sometimes possible to resist, as Nicholas I succeeded in doing, but lesser monarchs were forced to obey the pressure. In Norway the *Stor-*

thing abolished hereditary nobility in 1821. Fifteen years later it demanded further concessions, and Charles XIV of Sweden (the erstwhile Napoleonic general, Bernadotte) yielded in order to preserve the union of Norway and Sweden, easing the Act of 1814 that yoked the kingdoms. In Sweden likewise the intelligent monarch acknowledged the need for change; the educational system was expanded and liberalized, and the diet won control over the national revenues and asserted the principle of ministerial responsibility. In Denmark Frederick VI (1808–39) and Christian VIII (1839–48) still refused to compromise their absolutism by the grant of a constitution, but in the Netherlands the headstrong William I alienated his subjects so completely that they demanded legal restraints upon his power. Rather than accept a limited monarchy he abdicated in 1840 in favour of his more popular and more open-minded son, William II (1840–9). In Greece an insurrection forced Otto I, King of the Hellenes, to grant a constitution in 1843. In Switzerland a prolonged conflict between the conservatives and radicals, complicated by the rivalry of Catholics and Protestants, ended in 1847 with the victory of the Protestant cantons. The *Sonderbund* (a union of seven Catholic cantons formed in 1845) was dissolved, and the unity of the Swiss Confederation reaffirmed. The outcome was a victory of progressives over reactionaries, of those who favoured a stronger centralized confederation over those who wished to preserve cantonal autonomy.

Outside the Continent of Europe the development of greatest moment for the European peoples in these decades was the continued expansion of the United States of America. Between 1830 and 1850 its population almost doubled, rising from some twelve million to approximately twenty-three million. More extraordinary yet was the territorial expansion of the young giant of the west. The Louisiana Purchase of 1803 and the acquisition of Florida in 1819 had doubled its area, from 888,811 to 1,788,006 square miles. Between 1845 and 1848 the area almost doubled again to nearly 3,000,000 square miles. This sudden growth resulted from the annexation of Texas, a war with Mexico, and a treaty with Great Britain. Since 1836 Texas had maintained its independence of Mexican control, and in 1845 the United States Congress, by a simple majority vote, admitted 'the Republic of Texas' to the Union. A dispute with Mexico over the southern boundaries of the new state led to war the following year. When an expedition under General Winfield Scott occupied Mexico City the Mexican government abandoned the unequal struggle, ceding all claim not only to Texas but to New Mexico, Arizona, and California.

The United States election of 1844, which installed James K. Polk in the White House with a Congress pledged to 'the reannexation of Texas', had been waged with a second expansionist slogan: 'Fifty-four Forty or Fight!' For years the United States (under the vague definitions of the Louisiana Purchase) had advanced a claim to the Pacific coast area as far north as 54° 40′ north latitude, the point that demarcated the southern limit of the Russian territory of Alaska. Three European powers, however, still nursed claims to the Pacific slope of the North American continent. The Russians had founded posts as far south as California; Spanish navigators had explored the coast northward to Arctic waters; and the British advanced a title to all the coastal area north of the forty-second parallel. The Anglo-American rivalry was eased in 1818 by an accord that set the forty-ninth parallel as a boundary as far west as the Rocky Mountains, but beyond the mountains the Pacific coast from 42° northward was left open to joint occupancy. In 1819 the Spanish government resigned its tenuous claim on areas north of 42° to the United States; and in 1824 the Russians limited their southward advance to 54° 40'. American settlers now migrated in considerable numbers to the Oregon territory (there were 10,000 in the area by 1844), and the joint Anglo-American occupancy became impracticable. The difficulty was resolved by the Oregon treaty of 1846, which extended the boundary between the British and American lands westward along the forty-ninth parallel to the Pacific at the Gulf of Georgia. This clarification formally incorporated an area of 285,580 square miles within the boundaries of the United States. Added to the Texan territory assimilated in 1845 (390,144 square miles) and the Mexican cession of 1848 (529,017 square miles) these gains brought the United States an additional empire of 1,204,741 square miles in the three years from 1845 to 1848. This was almost one-third of the total area of Europe.

It was natural that the success of the democratic experiment in the New World should attract the attention of the Old: the Americans were heralds of the future. 'It appears to me beyond a doubt', Alexis de Tocqueville declared in 1835, 'that sooner or later we shall arrive, like the Americans, at an almost complete equality of conditions.' Tocqueville was the most profound observer to visit the United States in the first half of the nineteenth century, and his masterpiece, *La Démocratie en Amérique*, became a classic of liberal literature. 'I confess that in America I saw more than America', he wrote. 'I sought the image of democracy itself with its inclinations, its character, its prejudices, and its passions, in order to learn what we have to fear or to hope from its progress.' His liberal sympathies did not blind him to the faults and weaknesses in American society. He noted the hold that negro slavery maintained in the southern states and the disparity of economic development between the north and south. Within a century, he predicted, the United States would contain over a hundred million people, divided into forty states, and he concluded that, in these circumstances, 'the continuance of the Federal Government can only be a fortunate accident'. He admired the Americans, but he was often distressed by their vulgarity and appalled by their rapacity. 'Sometimes the progress of man is so rapid that the desert reappears behind him.' Despite their zeal for education and self-improvement the people of this new nation lacked a high intellectual tradition: 'America has hitherto produced very few writers of distinction; it possesses no great historians, and not a single poet.' But Tocqueville admitted the vitality and independence of the press and the vigour of public discussion. 'It is difficult to imagine the incredible rapidity with which public opinion circulates in the midst of these deserts.'

The republics of Latin America interested contemporary Europeans to a much feebler degree than the Anglo-American experiment in democracy. Observers could not penetrate the confused social castes nor comprehend the frequent political reversals that punctuated Latin American annals. The population south of the Rio Grande was of mixed origin, 45 per cent. Indian, 30 per cent. mestizos, 20 per cent. white, and 5 per cent. negro. The achievement of independence had not been followed, as in the United States, by the formation of a federal union; Bolivar's project for a great Spanish American confederacy had already miscarried before he died in 1830. Separatist movements and civil wars produced a score of jealous republics jostling one another for elbow room in a continent twice the area of Europe; and militarism and clericalism, negligible factors in North American society, remained constant forces in the politics of the Latin American states. The destiny thus decreed for the peoples of Central and South America largely isolated them from the world and from one another, but this segregation permitted them to develop unique cultural variations, offshoots of the European grafts on the ancient American Indian stem. The outcome was to be a rich flowering of original and sometimes exotic art and craftsmanship, but it was delayed—or rather due recognition of its novelty and variety was delayed—until the twentieth century.

The exodus of the Europeans into the semi-void areas

of the globe, which lured the North Americans to the Pacific, also gained momentum in other regions after 1830—in Canada, Australasia, and north-eastern Asia. The vast half-continent that was to become the Dominion of Canada held slightly more than a million people in 1830, but by 1848 the number had doubled. Antagonism between the French and British elements, and conflicts between the governing councils (members of which were appointed) and the popularly elected provincial assemblies sharpened to the point of open rebellion in 1837. The following year the Earl of Durham was sent from England as governor-in-chief to assess the causes of the discontent. His statesmanlike *Report on the Affairs of British North America* (1839) advocated the union of Upper and Lower Canada (Ontario and Quebec) and the establishment of responsible government. In 1840 the British Parliament passed the Act of Union, creating a single legislature for the two provinces with equal representation for each. Responsible government, though not specifically provided for in the Act, was achieved through successive precedents established in the ensuing decade.

British efforts to colonize Australia and New Zealand did not take positive form until the nineteenth century. The selection of New South Wales in 1788 as a place of exile for deported convicts deterred voluntary emigration, and only a few thousand free colonists arrived in Australia before 1830. But the profits of sheep raising and of wheat farming began to attract the adventurous, and after 1837 the transportation of felons was rapidly abandoned. Progressive steps towards colonial self-government were crowned by the Australian Colonies Government Act passed by the British Parliament in 1850, and the several states received the right to establish their own legislatures, expand the franchise, and adjust their tariffs. Tasmania, settled in 1803, was separated administratively from New South Wales in 1825, and later gained responsible government. The islands of New Zealand were not placed under British sovereignty until 1840, when the first shiploads of colonists arrived, and a constitution was granted the settlers in 1846. The almost unchallenged supremacy enjoyed by the British navy in the nineteenth century guarded the new and feeble colonies against attack by stronger powers, and British troops were available when needed to drive back the thinly scattered aborigines. Thus by the mid-nineteenth century, the continent of Australasia had become, in unspectacular fashion, a section of the British world empire. In their aggregate, Australia, Tasmania, and New Zealand exceeded 3,000,000 square miles, and were roughly equivalent to the recently expanded limits of the United States of America.

In yet a third continent, where sparsely scattered peoples could offer no effective resistance to European armies, the march of conquest and colonization proceeded inexorably in the second quarter of the nineteenth century. Between 1828 and 1846 the Kirghiz Steppe, a region stretching east from the Caspian Sea, three times the area of France, came under Russian domination. Still farther to the east and north, Russian military garrisons, convoys of prisoners condemned to hard labour, and thousands of labouring peasants built a route of empire to the Pacific between the fiftieth and sixtieth parallels of north latitude. Small, scattered outposts had been dotting this bleak Siberian wilderness by imperial ukase since the seventeenth century, and hardy fur traders had crossed the Bering Strait to Alaska in the 1780's. But the consolidation of this vast Russian realm in northern Asia required a permanent population. In 1850 a fortified settlement erected to guard the mouth of the Amur river was named Nikolayevsk in honour of the reigning Tsar, and ten years later Vladivostok, 'Conqueror of the East', was founded on the Sea of Japan. Russia was building bases that would project the Muscovite power into the Pacific Ocean.

In their conquering march through other continents the Europeans accepted their success as proof of the superiority of their institutions, their religion, and their culture. Yet it is doubtful if these advantages would have carried them far without the engines provided by a dynamic technology. The revolution wrought in transportation and communication by steam and electricity gave nineteenth-century expansion an irresistible momentum, equipping it with new nerves and new sinews. The triumphs of western technology, however, depended in turn on the development of a scientific mentality, and the influences that shaped the mind and spirit of western man were imponderable. In the scientific revolution instruments of precision were more important than instruments of power, and the most extraordinary intellectual innovation of recent times, 'the invention of invention', was no product of the machines. It presupposed a philosophical reorientation, a basic change of attitude and belief in the mind of the modern European. Throughout earlier ages philosophical speculation had proceeded from abstract premisses; it had developed as a part of a high intellectual tradition; it remained remote from mundane economy, much as man himself remained (in his own eyes) a special creation, in the world but not of it. The nineteenth century deserves to be considered the first century of the scientific age because its leading thinkers not only accepted the unity of the natural order, but also came to accept the fact that man himself formed a part of that order, subject to its laws and limitations.

The most helpful clue to nineteenth-century thought is this concept of *continuity*. Not merely historical continuity (a convenient argument against social revolution), but faith in continuity as a law of nature, affirming the existence of graduated, unbroken relationships throughout the world of experience. *Natura nil facit per saltum.* Divergencies or apparent discrepancies in the natural order could be reconciled (it was believed) by closer observation and more precise experiments. The aim of science was to bridge the gaps in human knowledge, working towards that synthesis where contradictories coincide.

Three notable conclusions in three separate fields, advanced between 1830 and 1848, helped to confirm this faith in the unity and continuity of nature. Sir Charles Lyell's *Principles of Geology* (1830–3) suggested that it was not necessary to invoke supernatural agencies or a succession of 'catastrophes' to explain the irregularities of the earth's surface. They could have been produced, Lyell submitted, by geological forces still at work, although this view assumed a much greater age for the earth than the few thousand years ascribed it by the chronology of the Scriptures. Thirty years were to pass before Lyell ventured to publish his conclusions on a more controversial subject, *The Antiquity of Man*, but by 1838 the researches of Mathias Jakob Schleiden already offered striking evidence on the unity of all living organisms. Schleiden stressed the importance of the nucleus in cell growth and the indispensable role of the cell as the fundamental unit in the structure of plants and animals. A third illustration of the economy and uniformity of nature was drawn, almost simultaneously, from the inorganic kingdom. Michael Faraday had shown as early as 1831 the possibility of electromagnetic induction. In 1840 the classical experiments of James Prescott Joule demonstrated the mechanical equivalent of heat in electrical and chemical change (Joule's law). The equivalence of heat and mechanical energy had already been elaborated mathematically by Sadi Carnot (1824), and the general principle of the conversion of energy, which came to be known as the Law of the Conservation of Energy, was summarized by Hermann Ludwig Ferdinand von Helmholtz in 1847.

It was understandable that problems of thermodynamics should fascinate a generation of scientists newly introduced to the efficacy of the steam-engine. The first railway—the Stockton and Darlington—was opened in

England in 1825. Four years later the earliest railways
built in France and the United States began operation.
Once instituted, the progress of the iron horse was
spectacular; by 1848 all northern Europe had been
joined together by metal links, and it was possible to
travel by rail from Paris to Hamburg, Dresden, Berlin,
Warsaw, and Vienna. The electric telegraph, developed
in practical form by the American inventor, Samuel
F. B. Morse, between 1832 and 1844, proved invaluable
in regulating railway traffic. On the oceans the advent
of steam and steel brought changes of equal moment.
Iron for shipbuilding was first introduced at Glasgow
in 1818 and the first screw propeller in 1836. The first
all-steam crossing of the Atlantic (by the Netherlands
steamer *Curaçao*) came in 1826. The Peninsula and
Oriental Line established regular steamship service
from England to Alexandria in 1839, and the first important transatlantic steamship line was founded by
Samuel Cunard in 1840.

With technological achievements so widespread and
so remarkable proclaiming the efficacy of applied science
it might be supposed that the literary interests of the
age would have taken a practical bent. But the opposite
was true; the intellectual impact of the new inventions
was delayed; and the European mentality in the second
quarter of the nineteenth century revealed a curious
dichotomy. Science, with its rational and positivist
approach, failed to capture the popular imagination.
Romanticism, with its emphasis on the emotional, the
imaginative, the supersensuous, and the supernatural,
dominated literature and the arts, and the western

world gave itself over to the pleasures of idealization and fantasy. The Germans and the British had already yielded to the new mood in the first quarter of the century, but the Latin peoples, more firmly wedded to neo-classical traditions, succumbed less readily. The growing popularity of Shakespeare in France after 1820 was a portent (as it had been in the Germanies fifty years earlier) that tastes were changing, and the disputes that raged over the virtues of Victor Hugo's *Hernani* on its presentation in 1830 proved that the Romantics could hold their own against the Classicists. In the subsequent decades the autobiographical novels of George Sand gained an extraordinary popularity in France and abroad. Her coterie included leading exponents of the Romantic movement from almost every field—Alfred de Musset in poetry, Balzac in fiction, Chopin in music, Delacroix in painting, Lamennais in religion. The Romantic spirit was at once egoistic and contagious, and its dominant drive was the urge to escape—into the anguish of a great passion, into far countries, into utopian dreams, into the past. Colourful historical romances had already become the most popular form of literature when Sir Walter Scott died in 1832. The more widely read historians of the age—Lamartine, Michelet, Macaulay, Carlyle—united the heart of the poet to the skill of the novelist. Victor Hugo's prolific output, that made him the undisputed monarch of Romantic literature for half a century, was a miscellany of poems, novels, histories, and political tracts, as rich in eloquence as they were barren in constructive ideas.

By the middle of the century every national literature of the western world had felt the impact of Romanticism although Germany, Britain, and France remained the mainsprings of the movement. In Russia Alexander Pushkin produced masterpieces in the Byronic style, in Italy Alessandro Manzoni's *I promessi sposi* (1827) took its place among the world's great romances, and in Spain and Portugal poets turned to Romantic themes under the inspiration of the French and German lyricists. Across the Atlantic the Romantic movement found its most individual expression in the fantastic melancholy of Edgar Allan Poe's verse, and in his prose *Tales of the Grotesque and Arabesque* (1840). In the field of the novel James Fenimore Cooper and Nathaniel Hawthorne completed their best work before 1850, and Herman Melville's classic, *Moby Dick*, appeared in 1851.

The fascination that rustic scenes, lonely ruins, misty mountains, and stormy skies held for the Romantic eye was early apparent in the landscapes of Casper David Friedrich in Germany and John Constable and J. M. W. Turner in England. Romantic painting in France was heralded by Jean Géricault and best exemplified in the canvases of Eugène Delacroix. The sculptors remained generally faithful to classical formulas through the first half of the nineteenth century—it was the era of Canova and Thorvaldsen—but in architecture the Romantic idealization of the Middle Ages inspired a Gothic revival. Ruined cloisters were rehabilitated; country homes were laid out with Gothic doorways and draughty baronial halls; and a battle of the styles developed between the protagonists of the Gothic revival and of the Classic tradition. In England the out-standing triumph of the Gothicists was represented by the Houses of Parliament (1840), and in France by the numerous reconstructions undertaken by Viollet-le-Duc, including the Sainte Chapelle at Paris and the walls of Carcassonne.

The music of the European people reflected the dominant influence of Romanticism throughout the nineteenth century. Its first quarter was the era of Beethoven, 'the Shakespeare of Music', of Carl Maria von Weber's fanciful operas, and of Schubert's exquisite songs. In all three composers the poetry and passion of the Romantic spirit could be heard transcending the more formal structure and regularity of the Classical idiom. Their deaths, within a few years of one another (1826-8), marked the transition to the second period of nineteenth-century music, a period distinguished by the work of Mendelssohn, Schumann, Chopin, Verdi, and, finally and pre-eminently, Wagner. Richard Wagner's prodigious influence on the modern opera was not yet widely felt by 1848, but his relationship to the Romantics was already evident in the style and themes of his *Tannhäuser* (1845) and *Lohengrin* (1848).

No one who ponders the art and literature of the time can fail to note how over-stimulated and confused the European imagination had become as the nineteenth century approached its middle point. The exaggeration, the mysticism, the cloudy perspectives, and the utopian dreams of the Romantic writers intensified the general mood of ardent aspiration for unattainable ends. It was a mood that largely ignored the world of practical affairs, a mood that was certain, when it invaded politics, to inspire idealistic programmes and feed upon extravagant promises. With the tide of liberalism rising throughout Europe and the social currents quickening toward revolution, it was almost inevitable that the journalists and poets, who had composed so many songs before sunrise, would be the first to harangue the masses from the barricades and proclaim Utopia in the forum. A new order was struggling to be born, but its self-appointed spokesmen had little understanding of its inner forces. The upheaval that impended in 1848 was to shake all Europe, prodigious in its prophecies but disappointing in its results, a fitting drama to close an age of Romantic frustration. Its defects were implicit in its leadership and in its appellation: it was to be 'the revolution of the intellectuals'.

F

Chapter Three

THE STRESS OF NATION-BUILDING
(1848–67)

IN 1848 as in 1830 the signal for a new wave of revolutionary outbreaks went out from Paris. Discontent had mounted during the 'hungry forties' in France as elsewhere, and the policy of immobility perfected by the government of the citizen king exasperated its critics. Yet the February revolution, deceptively swift and easy when it came, took the nation by surprise. On the 23rd of that month, crowds rioted before the home of the unpopular minister François Guizot; someone fired a pistol, the troops responded with a volley, and the demonstrators paraded the bodies of the dead through the streets to inflame the populace. Twenty-four hours later Louis Philippe abdicated, while the Chamber of Deputies proclaimed France a republic and appointed a provisional government.

From its earliest hours the Second French Republic was a house divided against itself; and it did not stand. The Right Wing in the provisional government (headed by the poet and historian Alphonse de Lamartine) desired a moderate middle-class republic. The Left Wing (best represented by the journalist and historian Louis Blanc) wanted far-reaching social and economic reforms. Both factions, moderate republicans and radical socialists, had united to overthrow the inert ministry of Guizot (yet another historian), but they could not unite to found a stable republic. In the first weeks after the coup of February 1848 Louis Blanc's influence appeared too strong to challenge; he was the author of a programme for a new social order which he had out-lined in his *Organisation du travail* (1840), and he had a large popular following. Pressed by the working men of Paris the provisional government established national workshops to assure jobs for all, and created a com-mission to reconcile the interests of employees and employers. But Paris was not France. The moderate republicans, relying on the more prudent mood of the nation, hastened the election of a national constituent assembly, and it was chosen by universal manhood suffrage on 23 April. The outcome was a clear vindi-cation for the centre and right; the moderate republi-cans could count on 500 of the 900 deputies. The second largest group were the monarchists; but they were divided into some 200 Orleanists, about 100 Legitimists, and a few Bonapartists. The Left Wing followers of Louis Blanc won less than a 100 seats.

In this register of national opinion the fate of the Second French Republic was already prefigured. The political revolution had been accepted by the nation as a *fait accompli*, but there was no real support for a social revolution outside the workers' *arrondissements* of Paris and the larger cities. The socialist agitators refused to accept the verdict of the electorate or to resign them-selves to an insignificant minority role in the Constitu-ent Assembly. Raising the cry 'bread or lead', the

Parisian proletariat staged a new insurrection (23–26
June), and the terrified bourgeoisie acclaimed General
Louis Cavaignac temporary dictator with orders to
subdue the populace. He succeeded; thousands died;
and the dream of class reconciliation that had been
proclaimed at the *Fete de la Concorde* a few weeks earlier
died with them.

'The red fool-fury of the Seine', as Tennyson termed
it, had been repressed once more, and the assembly
turned its attention to a constitution. A draft was
adopted 4 November 1848; it provided for a single
legislative chamber and a president, both elected by
universal manhood suffrage. Memories of the plebiscites that built a throne for the first Napoleon disquieted
a few shrewd deputies; but Lamartine rebuked them.
'Let God and the people decide', he insisted. On 10
December Prince Louis Napoleon Bonaparte, nephew
of the great emperor, was chosen president as nominee
of the 'Party of Order'. Although largely unknown, save
for his name and the fact that he had twice attempted
to seize power by still-born military coups, he received
over 5,000,000 of the 7,000,000 votes cast. Eight years
earlier, when the ashes of the first emperor were en-
tombed in the Invalides, Louis Blanc had warned
France against a Bonapartist restoration. 'It would be
the despotism without the glory, the courtiers on our
necks without Europe at our feet, a great name without
a great man, in a word, the Empire without the Emperor.' On 10 December 1848, the shadow of dictatorship fell across France, only a shadow as yet, but still
ominous. Louis Blanc, however, was no longer present

to repeat his warning; he had been driven into exile after the June Days.

History was to repeat itself, although, as Philip Guedalla has pointed out, the steps by which the prince-president retraced his uncle's course were less an example of historical repetition than of historical plagiarism. He reformed the ministry to secure a cabinet devoted to his own person; he discredited the legislators by appealing over their heads to the people; he revived martial hopes while insisting that he sought only the victories of peace. The constitution forbade a second consecutive term for the president, and after failing to secure an amendment Louis Napoleon and his intimate advisers prepared a *coup d'état*. It was sprung on 2 December 1851; leading journalists and deputies of the opposition were arrested in the night; a popular rising in the Faubourg Saint Antoine was crushed with considerable bloodshed; martial law was proclaimed in disturbed provinces; and Louis Napoleon announced that he had saved the liberties of the people. A plebiscite was held three weeks later, and the voters supported Napoleon (after the nation had been admonished that the alternatives were acquiescence or anarchy) by a majority announced as 7,500,000 to 640,000. On 2 December 1852, one year after the *coup d'état* and exactly forty-eight years after the coronation of the first Napoleon, a *senatus consultum* was promulgated establishing the Second Empire.

The political wheel had swung full circle since the early months of 1848, and the French people, recoiling before the vision of socialism and anarchism, had flung

themselves into the arms of a strong man. Four years
after the impatient Parisians had ejected Louis Philippe
because of the negative results of his domestic and
foreign policies, they found themselves subjected to a
dictatorship founded upon authoritarianism, militarism,
and clericalism. France had not passed through these
vicissitudes alone. Half the states of Europe evolved in
comparable fashion as the romance of 1848 was trans-
lated into the reality of 1850.

News of the February revolution in Paris traversed
Europe with remarkable speed, as if the newly developed
electric telegraph had linked the nerve-centres of the
nations and led them all to make a common response.
In Vienna, capital of reaction, a crowd stormed into the
diet on 13 March and then swept on to the Hofburg
where five demonstrators were killed in a collision with
the imperial guardians of order. The feckless Ferdinand I, baffled by the violence of his 'good Viennese',
hastened to appease them. Accepting the resignation of
Metternich, who left Austria, the emperor abolished
the censorship, approved the formation of a national
guard, and promised his subjects a constitution. But
the revival of popular disorders in May alarmed him
more deeply; he fled with the imperial family to Inns-
bruck; and a committee of public safety assumed
control in Vienna.

Throughout the Habsburg domains spontaneous uprisings rent the empire apart. The Hungarian diet
adopted an independent constitution (March Laws,
1848), and once again Ferdinand gave tacit approval.
The Croats organized a national committee pledged to

work for autonomy. The Czechs demanded a constituent assembly, and a Pan-Slav congress assembled at
Prague. Then the tide of revolution and separatism was
hurled backward as rapidly as it had risen. Prince
Alfred zu Windisch-Grätz, commanding the imperial
regiments at Prague, overthrew the revolutionary
Czech committee and set up a military government
(17 June). The octogenarian Marshal Joseph Radetzky
reasserted Austrian power in Lombardy and Venetia,
advancing from his bases in the Quadrilateral (Mantua,
Peschiera, Verona, and Legnano) to win a signal victory
over the Sardinian army at Custozza, 24 July. By
October the victorious military chiefs were dictating
Austrian policy, Baron Joseph Jellachich, governor of
Croatia, joined Windisch-Grätz before Vienna; they
bombarded and occupied the capital (31 October), and
executed the radical leaders.

In the face of these reverses the hope of reform faded,
and the springtime promises extracted from the irreso-
lute emperor became straw fetters to be brushed aside
by the batons of the victorious marshals. Radetzky
urged Ferdinand to resign in favour of his eighteen-
year-old nephew, Francis Joseph, who ascended the
imperial throne untrammelled by any constitutional
commitments. The chief minister of the young emperor was Prince Felix von Schwarzenberg, a forceful
diplomat who promulgated an emasculated constitution
by decree, and spurred the generals on to complete
the reconquest of Hungary. By January 1849, the imperial forces had re-entered Budapest. The defiant Hungarian diet, meeting elsewhere, proclaimed Hungary

a republic with Louis Kossuth as president, but the
new régime had little chance to survive in the wave
of reaction sweeping Europe in 1849. Its fate was sealed
by Nicholas I of Russia who dispatched an army to
complete its destruction. The Hungarian forces were
overwhelmed at Temesvar, on 9 August; Kossuth
escaped to Turkey; but a number of Hungarian
patriots, captured by the Austrian and Russian forces,
were hanged or shot in sanguinary reprisals. The Habsburg empire had been saved from dissolution at a
tragic price. Hopes for a healthy reorganization of the
monarchy, embodied by liberal thinkers in the still-
born Kremsier Constitution of March 1849, had failed,
and absolutism reappeared, softened by a few social
reforms. With successive attempts at repair, none of
which healed its fundamental weaknesses, the empire
on the Danube was to survive until 1918, just two
years longer than its new emperor, Francis Joseph
(1848-1916).

In the German states as in the Austrian lands Liberalism, Authoritarianism, and Nationalism clashed in 1848
with negative results, producing a confused, three-
sided contest. There was, however, one essential dif-
ference between the German states and the polyglot
empire of the Habsburgs. German nationalism was a
cohesive, not a disruptive, force; it was working to
create, not threatening to dissolve, an empire. When
Berlin was shaken by riots in March 1848, Frederick
William IV outdid himself with promises, pledging his
word that Prussia would be 'merged in Germany' under
a national constitution. Two months later a German

parliament of some 830 delegates, chosen by direct manhood suffrage, assembled at Frankfort-on-the-Main. This Frankfort Assembly faced a gigantic, possibly an insoluble, task. It sought to devise a constitution and government for a united Germany while four vital issues remained unsolved. (1) Should the new German Reich include the German provinces of Austria (the *Grossdeutsch* solution favoured by the Left) or omit them (the *Kleindeutsch* solution)? (2) Should non-German or part-German areas such as Prussian Poland, Bohemia, and Schleswig–Holstein be incorporated? (3) Should the new imperial constitution provide for a loose confederation of states or for a strongly centralized federal government? (4) Should the new Reich be a hereditary monarchy or a republic based upon the sovereignty of the people?

While the Frankfort delegates wrestled with these grave and intricate problems the march of events forced decisions upon them. The population of Schleswig and Holstein rebelled against Frederick VII of Denmark, and the Frankfort Assembly commissioned Prussia to intervene with armed forces, a patriotic rather than a parliamentary solution. When the recovery of Austria made it evident that the Habsburg court would oppose any Germanic union it could not dominate, the Frankfort Parliament reverted perforce to a *Kleindeutsch* formula, excluding Austrian provinces. The constitution adopted 27 March 1849 proposed a Federal Reich with a national parliament, under a hereditary emperor of the Germans, and Frederick William IV of Prussia was elected to this office. His refusal to accept an imperial crown from a popular assembly dealt a final blow to the entire project and discredited the Frankfort Parliament. Many moderate deputies went home in discouragement, and a radical minority adjourned to Stuttgart where their violent sessions were finally broken up by the Würtemberg soldiers (June 1849). The parliamentary approach to German unification had failed.

Had Frederick approved the constitution drafted by the Frankfort Parliament, he would have tacitly recognized the sovereignty of the German people. The jealousy of the Austrian court and the opposition of his brother-in-law, Nicholas I of Russia, reinforced his own innate distrust of democratic movements. But he still hoped to see a Germanic bloc take form in central Europe, embracing both Hohenzollern and Habsburg lands. Schwarzenberg at Vienna preferred to reconstitute the feeble diet of the German Confederation in which Austria had played a leading role. In the test of strength between the Berlin chancellery, with its plans for a Prussian Union, and the Austrian court with its determination to restore the settlement of 1815, Nicholas I gave his support to Vienna. Rather than risk war, Frederick William yielded, the tentative Prussian Union was dissolved, and the diet of the German Confederation re-established. Hohenzollern diplomacy had suffered a reverse commonly termed the Humiliation of Olmütz, and the Russian Tsar had proved in 1850 that he would oppose liberal trends in Germany as resolutely as he had fought republicanism in Hungary in 1849.

All the fervour, the fighting, the compromising and constitution-making of 1848–9 ended in central Europe with a virtual restoration of authoritarian principles. Liberal and national hopes had miscarried so completely that a profound bitterness and disillusionment swept German intellectual circles. Some ardent reformers, like the young Carl Schurz, emigrated to the United States, persuaded that the flower of freedom could not blossom on the poisoned soil of Europe. Others, who remained, tried to find consolation in the meagre gains that had been achieved. In Prussia a limited constitution, elaborated after 1849, provided for a bicameral legislature with the lower house chosen by universal manhood suffrage. But the voters were divided into three classes according to their tax-paying ability, and the two wealthier groups, although they constituted only 17 per cent. of the electorate, chose two-thirds of the deputies. This Prussian Landtag could approve new laws, but it could not choose the ministers of the king; and the latter could rule by decree when the parliament was not in session.

For patriotic Germans the frustration of national hopes was a sharper disappointment than the miscarriage of liberal aspirations. It is significant that a majority of the Frankfort delegates had revealed, often unthinkingly, their willingness to compromise democratic principles in order to promote national aims; their tragedy lay in the fact that they achieved neither. The legend was later to find general acceptance that 1848 marked a turning-point in German destiny, and that the defeat of the Frankfort programme delivered

the German people over to Bismarck and the cult of
national egoism. Yet it seems clear that national egoism
was already a dominant force in 1848. However elo-
quently the middle-class leaders at Frankfort might
denounce autocracy, their votes proved that they were
ever ready to invoke authoritarian aid, whether to
secure Schleswig–Hostein, to hold the Polish provinces,
to conquer Bohemia, or to crush the rebellious Slavs.
The radicals allied themselves with the Pan-Germans
whenever it was a question of preserving scattered
German communities from absorption by the non-
German majorities in the border regions.

The judicious Heinrich von Gagern, president of the
Frankfort Parliament, spoke the thought of the majority
when he proclaimed: 'What unity must we seek? That
we live up to the destiny laid on us in the east; that we
embrace as satellites in our planetary system those
peoples in the Danube Basin who have no talent for and
no claim to independence.' Such denial of self-deter-
mination to others by an assembly that rested its own
authority on a popular mandate disclosed a paralysing
contradiction in ideals. For the peoples with 'no claim
to independence' were in revolt; they could be held
only by force; and force lay with the generals. By
January 1849 even the radicals at Frankfort were ready
to applaud a deputy who declared: 'I would cheerfully
renounce all our theorems and articles to found a great,
powerful, and dominant Reich, led by Austria and her
great generals, Radetzky, Windisch-Grätz, and Jellachich. . . . Let us first found real power, and then
establish freedom, which is impotent without power.'

For 'Austria' it is necessary to read 'Prussia'—the speaker was citing the right script in wrong characters. Yet his intuition was unerring. The German generation that came of age in 1848 rode forth on a romantic quest to rescue liberty. They turned back to marry power.

In Italy as in central Europe the hopes of 1848 were darkened by the events of 1849. The deferment of Italian political unity was the more surprising because the Alps and the sea made the peninsula a geographical entity. 'Italy is one nation', Napoleon I had pointed out thirty years earlier. 'Unity of customs, language, and literature must, at a period more or less distant, unite her inhabitants under one government, and Rome will without doubt be chosen by the Italians as their capital.' All roads led to Rome, but in 1848 the Italians had not yet decided which one they would follow. Giuseppe Mazzini, exiled after the Revolution of 1830, had dedicated himself and his 'Young Italy' to the dream of a unitary, secular republic. Vincenzo Gioberti, likewise in exile, proposed a confederation of all Italian states with the Pope as president. 'Italy is the true head of civilization and Rome is the ideal metropolis of the world', he wrote in his *Moral and Civil Primacy of the Italians* (1843). To many Italian Catholics, Gioberti's plan offered the most promising solution to the 'Roman Question' because it was improbable that the Pope would resign his temporal authority on any other terms, or willingly see Rome and the papal domains absorbed into a secular territorial state. A third programme for unification, intermediate between the two, proposed the formation of a national, monarchical state with the head of the house of Savoy as king of a united Italy. This plan found favour with many liberal intellectuals and business men who realized that Piedmont–Sardinia was the most advanced state in Italy economically and that Charles Albert of Savoy was in the best position to drive the Austrian garrisons from their positions in the Po valley.

Italy was already seething with unrest from Milan to Naples when the news arrived in March 1848 that Metternich had fled from Vienna and Austria was in the throes of dissolution. Spontaneous uprisings in Venice and Milan drove out the Austrian whitecoats, and at Turin Charles Albert, with belated zeal, ordered the Sardinian army to support the national crusade. Popular enthusiasm at Rome and Naples moved Pius IX and Ferdinand II to send detachments to harry the retreating Austrians. *L'Italia farà da se*, Charles Albert proclaimed, and a wave of patriotic enthusiasm swept the peninsula. But events swiftly proved that Italy could not 'do it herself'. Divided counsels, dilatory tactics, and growing rifts among the revolutionary factions paralysed the patriotic cause. The papal and Neapolitan columns were recalled in May, and Radetzky, rallying the Austrian forces, defeated Charles Albert at Custozza (24 July 1848). The Italian operations had been weakened by dissension from the first; and as the weeks passed the moderate revolutionaries became dismayed by the increasing violence of the radicals. At Rome a popular insurrection drove Pius IX from the city and a republic was proclaimed with Mazzini as its moving spirit and the tireless knight of liberty, Giuseppe

Garibaldi, as its defender. But Naples had already yielded to reaction, and French and Austrian armies were preparing to dispute for control of a still divided Italy.

The Austrians moved first. On 23 March at Novara Radetzky inflicted a second and more crushing defeat on Charles Albert, who abdicated in favour of his son Victor Emmanuel II. In April a French expedition disembarked at Civita Vecchia and laid siege to Rome; the republicans were driven out, and Pius IX returned cured of his liberal sympathies. In May Austrian reinforcements restored the Grand Duke Leopold to power in Florence, and in July a second Austrian force bombarded Venice until the cholera-stricken city surrendered. By the close of 1849 the revolutionary movement had been crushed; Mazzini and Garibaldi were once more in exile; the military ineptitude and lack of unity that weakened the Italian revolutionaries had been revealed to the world and the republican cause completely discredited. Despite the presence of a French garrison at Rome that stayed to guard the papal possessions, the Austrian influence had been restored in Italy as effectively as in the Germanies.

The developments of 1848–9 taught the same lesson in various forms throughout continental Europe. When faced with the alternative, a majority of the people would endure despotism and militarism rather than embrace the cause of revolution. There was, however, a discernible shift in the centre of authority; absolute monarchy was changing by revolution or by evolution to constitutional monarchy; the power of the hereditary

land-owning aristocracy was in decline; and the power
of the bourgeoisie was rising—was already, in Britain,
France, and Belgium, the dominant influence in the
state. But the franchise still rested upon tax or property
qualifications, political power remained with the middle
and upper classes, and though they might dispute on
occasion they wielded it jointly in defence of their
common interests. The essential clause in the bourgeois
constitutions of the nineteenth century was the sacred-
ness of private property. When this clause was called
in question the typical bourgeois liberal reacted like a
typical conservative. He might defend political equality
in theory, but he would not promote economic egali-
tarianism in fact.

The most unmanageable factor in the bourgeois-
dominated society was the industrial machine, for the
machine was not only multiplying the profits of the
factory owner, it was also multiplying the number of
discontented proletarians. To meet this growing menace
the first half of the nineteenth century produced no
satisfactory solution. Most social thinkers of that age
who recognized the problem at all preferred to expound
romantic cures rather than to cope with economic
realities. Their 'systems' were intellectual exercises that
failed in application and earned for their advocates the
derisive title of 'utopian socialists'. Most ideological of
these major prophets of a new order was François Marie
Charles Fourier (1772–1837). Fourier urged the organization of individual communities (*phalanstères*) of
1,620 members, each participant labouring according
to his aptitudes and inclinations so that none would

feel constrained and a spirit of complete harmony would prevail. Fundamentally, the pattern he advocated was a form of agrarian communism; and although attempts to apply it failed in France, several experimental colonies on Fourierist lines were founded in the United States. More realistic, in the sense that he accepted the decisive role of science and industry in modern society, was the socialism of Claude Henri de Rouvroy, Comte de Saint-Simon (1760–1825). His ideal order provided for a new social system of three classes: priests, savants, and industrials. The priests were to be at once moral leaders, artists and guardians of the (Saint-Simonian) dispensation. The savants were to be scientists, teachers, and philosophers. The industrials, the most numerous class, were to be employed and cared for under a regimen that approximated to state socialism. The weakness of these schemes, and of others, less noteworthy, that attracted attention in the decades before 1848, lay in their assumption that human passions could be harmonized, and social antagonisms could be healed, by a philosophic formula. They were panaceas for perpetual peace drafted by doctrinaires while the opposing armies formed their lines for a century of social conflict.

The fundamental cleavage in European society had ceased, by the middle of the nineteenth century, to be the historical distinction between a privileged aristocracy and priesthood and the great body of unprivileged commoners. It had become instead a cleavage between those with property and those without, between those who owned the machinery of production and those who

G

worked it, between employers and employees, in a word, between the bourgeoisie and the proletariat. This class conflict Karl Marx and Friedrich Engels exaggerated in memorable and dogmatic phrases in their *Communist Manifesto* of 1848 and later elaborated in the three volumes of *Das Kapital* (1867–95).

The history of all hitherto existing societies [they wrote, in 1848] is the history of class struggles. . . . Society as a whole is more and more splitting up into two great hostile camps . . . Bourgeoisie and Proletariat. . . . The executive of the modern State is but a committee for managing the common affairs of the whole bourgeoisie. . . . Let the ruling classes tremble at a Communistic revolution. The proletarians have nothing to lose but their chains. They have a world to win.

Working men of all countries, unite!

The Communist League, an international socialist organization that had commissioned Marx and Engels to draft this defiant proclamation, was disbanded in the reaction after 1848. For decades militant communism remained a shadow without much substance; Marx himself had described it as a spectre; yet it was a spectre that haunted Europe thenceforward. With the appearance of the Communist manifesto the era of utopian socialism declined. After 1848 socialists found that a change had come over the spirit of their dream, and the middle classes grew more acutely conscious of the rising threat from below. The frightened bourgeois had seen the proletarians throw up barricades; the barricades had fallen but the memory lived; and sober men of property sought for surer methods to restrain the restless masses. The middle classes realized somewhat late that ideas were weapons in the class war, and that in weakening the authority of organized religion they had reduced the influence of the clergy, the 'spiritual gendarmes' who might have guarded the populace against the infection of 'social heresies'. Ruling groups, even in Protestant countries, turned a more favourable gaze upon the Catholic Church after 1848. The Papacy concluded new concordats with the governments of Spain and Austria; Louis Napoleon strengthened the influence of the Church in France; and Catholic hierarchies were re-established in England (1850) and the Dutch Netherlands (1853). After the outbreaks of 1848, as in 1815, governments labouring to restore their shaken authority recognized that religion was an efficacious antidote to that revolutionary malady which had proved so dangerously contagious.

Another and more effective antidote to popular discontent was the rapid improvement in economic conditions that came after 1848. The poor crops, the hunger, and the unemployment of the 1840's had fostered revolt; the business expansion of the 1850's brought more prosperous times and some of the benefit filtered down to the depressed classes. Emigration overseas, a ready barometer of economic distress, had quadrupled in the ten years before 1850, but after that date it declined from a peak of some 400,000 annually to approximately 200,000. The causes of business fluctuations remained something of a mystery, but a sufficient body of statistics had accumulated by 1850 to demonstrate that world trade was increasing with unexampled rapidity—it was to double on an average once every twenty years throughout the remainder of the century. Economic progress, however, remained subject to disconcerting leaps and pauses. One explanation offered for the sudden expansion in the early 1850's was the discovery of gold deposits in California (1848) and in Australia (1851) which increased the supply of monetary gold, the world total rising 5 per cent. per annum from 1848 to 1857. Britain led the economic advance, exports from the United Kingdom increasing by one-third between 1850 and 1855; but mechanization of industry also made notable gains in France, and spread from its older centres in Prussia and Saxony to all the states of the Germanies. The mining of coal, smelting of iron, and construction of railways proceeded with extraordinary energy, and manufacturers' profits were magnified by the heavy expenditures of the British and French governments resulting from their war in the Crimea (1854–6). After the war ended, the period of prosperity culminated suddenly in 1857 with a sharp recession that affected Europe and America simultaneously, the first financial panic that may truly be called a world-wide economic crisis. It was evidence of the growing interdependence of world markets and an omen of the increasingly severe depressions that were to follow periods of over-expansion in the future.

During thirty-nine years, from 1815 to 1854, the great European powers had avoided any armed clash among themselves. This long peace was shattered by the outbreak of the Crimean War in 1854, and the seventeen years from 1854 to 1871 brought five separate conflicts each of which involved two or more great powers. Following this militant interlude there was to be another unusually long period of peace, from 1871 to 1914, during which no first-class powers engaged one another in battle on European soil.

France and Britain blundered into war with Russia in 1854 through a series of tragic misunderstandings, the responsibility for which was shared by all the governments concerned. Fear of the Muscovite giant haunted the dreams of British statesmen throughout the nineteenth century, for Russian encroachments were a growing threat to the Turkish empire, to Persia, and to British control of India. When the rigid Nicholas System preserved Russia unshaken through the revolutionary years 1848-9 the Tsarist empire emerged with prestige enhanced by its apparent strength and stability. While France, Austria, and Prussia were distracted by internal disorders, Russian forces moved into the Danubian principalities (Moldavia and Wallachia). Although this occupation of territories nominally subject to the sultan was undertaken with the latter's consent, and the Russian troops were withdrawn in 1851, the British, French, and Austrian governments watched with disquiet the growth of Russian influence in the Balkans. To diplomats in London and Paris especially the events of 1848-9 brought a sense of discomfiture. The Second French Republic could not pursue a firm foreign policy because it was at best a provisory régime, and the British, with a powerful navy but a negligible army, could not easily apply pressure against the eastern European powers. Palmerston's efforts to intercede on behalf of the Danes, the Hungarians, and the Italian liberals were rebuffed, while Nicholas of Russia used military and diplomatic pressure to influence developments in central Europe. The long-standing opposition between the autocratic (eastern) bloc and the liberal (western) nations thus furnished a strong argument for Franco-British unity.

France and Russia had conflicting interests in the Near East, where both powers claimed the right to protect Christian minorities and Christian pilgrims in the Holy Land. With the establishment of the Second Empire in 1852 this dispute became sharper, but Nicholas believed he could afford to ignore French protests. Since 1833 (treaty of Unkiar Skelessi) Russian influence had been dominant at Constantinople, and Russian diplomats had reached secret accords with the Austrian and British governments for the ultimate division of the Ottoman empire. The Anglo-Russian agreement had been formulated when the Tsar visited London in 1844, and confirmed though not clearly defined in a memorandum drafted by the Russian chancellor, Carl Robert Nesselrode. In 1852 the Russian diplomats still counted upon British willingness to accept Crete and Egypt as compensation if Russia annexed Turkish territory in Europe, but this scheme for an Anglo-Russian settlement of the Near Eastern question collapsed suddenly and irretrievably in March 1853. Without warning, the British foreign secretary informed the Tsar that the (still secret) accord drafted nine years earlier was unsatisfactory. In this reversal of policy the cabinet at London was influenced by two major considerations, the continued evasiveness of the Russians regarding the disposition to be made of Constantinople and the Straits, and a sharp though indirect warning through Brussels that if French interests were disregarded in the Near East a French army would occupy Belgium as compensation. Placed in a situation where they must alienate Russia or antagonize France, the British cabinet made a swift decision, sending a naval squadron to join the French Mediterranean fleet at the entrance to the Dardanelles. The two maritime powers then advised the sultan's government to defy Russian threats.

Nicholas felt that he had gone too far to retreat with dignity; his army was already massed on the Turkish border. By July 1853 the Russians had once again overrun the Danubian Principalities; attempts by the Austrian court to arbitrate the issue broke down; and in September the British fleet moved on to Constantinople. Encouraged by this evidence of support, the Turks declared war on Russia, the allied navies entered the Black Sea, and on 28 March 1854, France and Britain declared war on Russia. Nicholas then accepted an ultimatum he had ignored earlier, and his forces, which had already crossed the Danube, were withdrawn from the Principalities, ending the Balkan phase of hostilities. But the Allies were not ready for peace; they transferred the scene of battle to the Crimean peninsula where an Anglo-French expeditionary force laid siege to the Russian fortifications at Sevastopol. In December 1854 Austria joined in a defensive and offensive alliance with France and Britain, but refrained from hostilities, and the siege of Sevastopol continued with heavy casualties until the Russians evacuated the city on 11 September 1855. Nicholas I had died the previous March and his successor, Alexander II, was a man of more pliant character. A threat from Vienna that Austria would enter the war persuaded the Russian government to accept peace, and the terms of settlement were arranged at the Congress of Paris, 25 February–30 March 1856.

Few wars in history had revealed more confusion of purpose, more incompetence in command, more costly casualties, and more negative results. The sultan preserved his empire for the moment and made promises of reforms which he did not fulfil. The Russians abandoned their conquests and agreed to neutralize the Black Sea, but evaded these restrictions after fourteen years. The Principalities were placed under a joint guarantee of the powers which was modified within a generation; and Britain, France, and Austria promised to guard and maintain the integrity of the Turkish empire, a pledge they all found it inexpedient to keep. For this inconclusive result over a quarter of a million men had died of battle or disease. The Concert of Europe had broken down, in part because Napoleon III had hoped to force a general reconsideration of the Vienna Settlement of forty years earlier. Indirectly, however, the Crimean War helped to promote two developments in international affairs that must be accounted benefits, though these grew out of the conduct of the war and had no relation to its causes. By the Declaration of Paris (1856) the powers established international rules to govern maritime blockade, protect neutral rights, and abolish privateering. The sufferings endured by the soldiers also awakened wide concern, and this helped to bring about the formation of the International Red Cross, established in 1864 by the Geneva Convention. The conscience of the western world had been shocked by the dispatches of war correspondents on the Crimean front who revealed the misery to which the troops were exposed from the icy weather, gangrene, pneumonia, typhus, and cholera. The commissariat and medical services of all the belligerents had proved shamefully inadequate, and four-fifths of the war deaths were the result of disease.

In the later phases of their war with Russia the British, French, and Turkish forces had been supported by 10,000 soldiers dispatched by the kingdom of Sardinia. This north Italian state had no real quarrel with Russia, but Victor Emmanuel II and his astute minister, Camillo di Cavour, hoped to win Anglo-French gratitude and to bring up the Italian question at the peace table. These hopes were not realized at the Congress of Paris, and Cavour then concentrated on winning the aid of Napoleon III with whom he entered into secret negotiations two years later. The emperor promised that if Austria attacked Sardinia a French army of 200,000 men would cross the Alps and Italy would be freed 'from the Alps to the Adriatic'. Louis Napoleon did not intend to promote a united kingdom of Italy; the plan provided that Piedmont–Sardinia might annex Lombardy–Venetia, Parma, Modena, and the Legations;

that Tuscany, the Marches, and Umbria would be merged into a central Italian state; that the Pope would retain Rome and the Campagna; and the kingdom of Naples would remain intact. The four political segments might then be joined in a loose confederation with the Pope as president. On 23 January 1859, the French and Sardinian statesmen amplified their accord with a military convention. As compensation for the assistance promised, France was to receive Savoy and Nice from Sardinia.

In its execution the initial plan rapidly outran Napoleon's calculations. Cavour successfully provoked Austria, and the governing group at Vienna obligingly provided a *casus belli* by opening hostilities against the Sardinian kingdom at the end of April 1859. The first major battle took place on 4 June at Magenta; the Austrians withdrew in defeat; and a second sanguinary engagement at Solferino on 24 June induced both leading belligerents to consider peace. Napoleon III was depressed by the slaughter, disconcerted by the movement for national unification that was sweeping Italy, and fearful that Prussia might join Austria and attack France directly. Without consulting his Sardinian allies, the emperor concluded a truce with Francis Joseph at Villafranca on 11 July. Cavour was anxious that Sardinia should continue the fight alone; he therefore resigned from office when the more realistic Victor Emmanuel accepted the disappointing peace. Lombardy was transferred to Sardinia, but Venetia remained under Austrian control. After plebiscites, and amid great popular enthusiasm, Parma, Modena, the Romagna, and Tuscany were joined to the Sardinian kingdom. In their eagerness to win all Italy the partisans of union then turned to Naples and Rome. Garibaldi, with his famous thousand, disembarked in Sicily, secured the island in a few weeks, and crossed to Naples where he was welcomed as a liberator. He was about to march on Rome when Cavour, who had returned to office, forestalled such a brusque solution of the Roman question, fearing it might bring the Catholic powers to the aid of Pius IX. Piedmontese troops entered the domains of the Church and dispersed a papal force at Castelfidardo, but they spared Rome and moved south to unite with Garibaldi's hot-headed volunteers and take the initiative from them. By the close of 1860 Naples, Sicily, the Marches, and Umbria had joined the new kingdom of Italy. It was formally proclaimed on 17 March 1861, with Victor Emmanuel as king and the Piedmontese *Statuto* of 1848 as a constitution.

The stupendous exertions of these final months had overtaxed Cavour. He died on 6 June 1861, consoled by the assurance that *L'Italia è fatto*. Italy was made, but it was not yet complete. Rome remained a papal city defended by a French garrison, and the whitecoats still held Venetia. It was necessary for the Italians to fight the Austrians once more in 1866 (this time with Prussia as an ally) before the ancient republic of the doges could be added to the new Italian kingdom. Rome was not entered until the French garrison withdrew in 1870, after which the troops of Victor Emmanuel breached the walls and Pius IX shut himself in the Vatican, his temporal sovereignty wrested from him by the secular power. These later events were epilogues to the essential drama of Italian unification which had reached its climax in the deciding years 1859–61. The forces of Italian nationalism had triumphed over Austrian antagonism and papal resistance, and three men of different character but equal patriotism had prepared the victory, Mazzini the soul, Garibaldi the sword, and Cavour the brain of the *risorgimento*.

The part played by the kingdom of Piedmont–Sardinia in forging Italian unity revived the ardour of those nationalists who hoped to see Prussia play a comparable role in the Germanies. There too Austria stood for separatism and particularism, and it was clear from the events of 1848–50 that Austria would fight to prevent the organization of a German federal state under Prussian leadership. The realistic statesmen at Berlin were ready to settle the issue on the battlefield, and they were determined that Prussia, unlike Sardinia, should 'do it herself', for the price of French or Russian aid might prove too high. In 1859, while he was still regent, the new Hohenzollern ruler, William I (1861–88), appointed Albert von Roon minister of war and Helmuth von Moltke chief of staff, with instructions to strengthen the Prussian army. The opposition of the liberal majority in the Landtag almost halted the programme in 1862, but William found a leader for his council of ministers who was prepared to override parliamentary objections. The man he turned to was Otto von Bismarck, an arrogant, adroit, and unscrupulous statesman, who frankly avowed his contempt for Austrian ineptitude and for parliamentary vacillation, and insisted that the great questions of the day would be decided by 'blood and iron'.

In 1864 the reorganized Prussian army received its baptism of fire during a short war with the Danes. Frederick VII, counting on British and Swedish support, had sought to incorporate the duchy of Schleswig into the Danish kingdom, a policy reaffirmed by his successor, Christian IX. The status of Schleswig and Holstein was extraordinarily complicated; both were possessions of the Danish crown, but Holstein was a member of the German Confederation. Resorting to arms, Austria and Prussia defeated the Danes and occupied both duchies, compelling Christian IX to relinquish them (peace of Vienna, 1864). Austria proceeded to administer Holstein while Prussia took Schleswig, a solution certain to provoke difficulties because Hostein was virtually an enclave within Prussian territory, and the Zollverein (the Prussian-dominated customs union) had been expanded in 1853 to embrace all non-Austrian German states. In October 1865 Bismarck secured a promise from Napoleon III that France would observe neutrality in the event of a war between Austria and Prussia, Napoleon accepting vague assurances of 'compensations'. With Russia Bismarck had already established cordial relations (he had served as ambassador to Saint Petersburg from 1859 to 1862), and in April 1866 he concluded an alliance with the Italian kingdom which was to annex Venetia if Austria were defeated. These diplomatic preliminaries completed, Prussia precipitated war by moving troops into the duchy of Holstein (June 1866).

Austria appealed to the diet of the German Confederation, and most of the German states took the Austrian side. But the issue was decided in a few weeks by the rapidity and success of the Prussian military moves. Moltke shattered the Austrian army in Bohemia in a single decisive battle at Königgrätz (or Sadowa) on 3 July 1866. Prussian breech-loading rifles proved their lethal efficiency against the Austrian muzzle loaders, and Moltke's use of railways for troop transport revolutionized strategy. The timing of the Prussian stroke had been masterly; for the Austrians, who had vanquished the Italian army decisively at Custozza on 24 June, could have recalled sufficient forces to change the military balance in the north if they had been given a few more days.

Bismarck made peace as swiftly as he had made war. The Italians received Venetia despite their military defeat at Custozza and a naval defeat at Lissa. Before Napoleon III could revise his diplomacy to match events (he had counted on a protracted war and an Austrian victory) the treaty of Prague was signed on 23 August 1866. The German Confederation was at an end, and Austria was excluded from Germany. All states north of the Main river joined a North German Confederation under Prussian leadership and the south German states were left independent. When Napoleon III claimed some measure of compensation for France, his ambassador, Vincent Benedetti, imprudently put the French demands for Luxemburg and Belgium in writing. Bismarck revealed this proof of French aggressiveness to the diplomats of the south German states,

Baden, Würtemberg, and Bavaria, which thereupon joined the Zollverein and concluded military alliances with Prussia. In their new independence (and isolation) their fear of France was greater than their distrust of Prussia.

At Paris the consequences of the Seven Weeks War of 1866 excited anger and mortification. Sadowa, it was now admitted, had been a defeat for the French because they were not there. Napoleon III had been guilty of costly miscalculations, not the least being his estimate of Bismarck, formed in 1862 when the latter was ambassador to Paris. After frequent conversations he concluded that the tall Prussian was 'not serious'. Bismarck had shown more insight. He decided that the enigmatic nephew of the great Napoleon was a sphinx without a riddle, 'a great, unrecognized incapacity'.

The Seven Weeks War settled the major problems of German unification; subsequent developments merely confirmed and extended that settlement. The constitution of the North German Confederation provided for federal union in which the component states retained their own administration but the federal government controlled foreign policy and the direction of the military forces. The King of Prussia became commander-in-chief and President of the Federation; in the federal council (Bundesrat) Prussia controlled seventeen of the forty-three votes and could block amendments as these required a two-thirds majority. The lower house (Reichstag), which was elected by universal manhood suffrage, provided a concession to liberal opinion without threatening Bismarck's ascendency; for the chancellor of the North German Confederation was to be responsible to the king of Prussia, not to the Reichstag and this key post Bismarck reserved for himself. His quarrel with the Prussian parliament had been healed at the close of 1866 when a majoirty of the liberals approved a Bill of Indemnity, thus giving assent retroactively to acts they had declared arbitrary and illegal but now applauded when they saw them crowned with success.

For the Habsburgs the Seven Weeks War meant the end of their historic role in Italian and German politics. More than this, it meant that the bureaucrats at Vienna must face the necessity of reorganizing the internal administration of the Habsburg empire. Autocracy, restored after the revolts of 1848, had functioned for a decade; but the Italian war of 1859 and the defeat of Königgrätz in 1866 discredited the régime at Vienna and the army that was its mainstay. Francis Joseph could no longer evade the fact that he must surrender some of his prerogatives and modify the fundamental laws of the absolute monarchy.

The Compromise (*Ausgleich*) of 1867 was the consequence. Since 1860 the young emperor had experimented tentatively with a shadow parliament, a Reichsrath, but the Hungarian deputies withdrew in 1861 and the Czechs protested that it was another 'Germanizing' move of the imperial bureaucracy. Some form of decentralization, of federalism, appeared unavoidable, but if all the national minorities in the Habsburg lands were granted local autonomy the empire would be transformed into a confederation of

eight or nine segments. The solution Francis Joseph
adopted preserved the dominant position of the German
minority in Austria and recognized that of the Magyar
minority in Hungary. Under the Dual Monarchy
established in 1867 Hungary became an independent
kingdom with its own capital, its own parliament, and
its own ministry. The two halves of the empire were
linked by the fact that Francis Joseph was Emperor of
Austria and King of Hungary, while such common
problems as foreign affairs, defence, and finance were
adjusted through delegations from the two parliaments.
Tariff and economic issues were settled by an accord
between Austria and Hungary renewable every ten
years.

The gravest defect of the dual system was its failure
to placate the minority peoples, especially the Slavs.
Czech patriots demanded indignantly that the ancient
kingdom of Bohemia be re-created and granted the
same semi-independent status as Hungary. The
Slovenes dreamed of uniting with Croats and Serbs to
form an independent Yugoslav kingdom. Italian-speak-
ing residents of Trieste and Istria looked towards Italy,
and Rumanian nationalists in Bukovina towards
Rumania. These discontented minorities made it very
difficult for Francis Joseph to introduce genuine
representative government lest the Germans in Austria
and the Magyars in Hungary be outvoted by the combined opposition. In Hungary the Magyars limited the
franchise to less than one-twentieth of the population.

The Poles living under Austrian rule were less dissatisfied than most of their fellow Slavs. They realized

H

that the reconstitution of Poland as an independent state was an almost unattainable ideal, and as Catholics they found some compensation in the fact that (unlike their Prussian and Russian brothers) they were subjects of a Catholic monarch. Furthermore, Francis Joseph allowed them a small degree of freedom in managing their own affairs and permitted them to keep alive their cultural if not their national aspirations. But perhaps the shrewdest policy adopted by the Austrian government was to subordinate the Ruthenians to the Poles. To maintain this relative superiority and hold their own against the Czechs the Poles accepted their own subordination to Vienna.

In Russia as in Austria military defeats shook the prestige of the autocracy and the army and brought fundamental changes in the system of government. During the decade that followed the Crimean War the new Tsar, Alexander II (1855–81), introduced a series of reforms, the most important being the abolition of serfdom. Nine-tenths of the Russian soil was still in the possession of the state and the noble families in the middle of the century, and on this land lived 47,000,000 serfs, bound to the soil or to personal service. After cautious preparation Alexander issued an Emancipation Proclamation in 1861. All serfs gained their personal freedom, and those on the soil received farmland to work for themselves. The imperial government assumed responsibility for the compensation paid to the noble landholders, and as free peasants the former serfs were to reimburse the government by redemption payments spread over a period of forty-nine years. The solution had inevitable defects, and some critics complained that the serfs merely exchanged masters, becoming serfs of the state until they worked out their long redemption. Despite objections, Alexander held on his course; and while his zeal lasted he introduced other courageous reforms, seeking the approval of the 'westernizers' who wished Russia to imitate the more advanced institutions of the leading European states. New courts of justice were established in 1862, education was fostered, and local assemblies (zemstvos) were promised to each provincial district, the members to be elected by indirect suffrage (1864). Unfortunately, the outbreak of a revolution in Poland (1863) daunted the Tsar Liberator, and as his ardour for experiments declined the Slavophils regained their influence. They had always considered the civilization of Holy Russia a unique culture, and they believed that Russian society should be left to evolve according to its own social and religious patterns, and should not have western traditions forced upon it. By 1867 the ideals of Orthodoxy, Autocracy, and Nationalism were regaining their influence and the hope of further reforms waned, but the Emancipation edict remained the most momentous event in Russian national life in the nineteenth century.

To Great Britain the middle years of the nineteenth century brought domestic tranquillity, increasing prosperity, and a world-wide prestige. The bourgeois fear of radical working-class movements abated after 1848, partly because the trade-union leaders showed themselves prudent and moderate in their demands. The workers gained concessions from their employers by direct bargaining, and the collapse of the Chartist Movement left them apathetic on most political issues. On occasion, however, working-class pressure made itself felt and influenced government policy. Throughout the American Civil War of 1861–5 British upperclass opinion tended to favour the Confederacy, but radical and liberal groups regarded the Union forces as the forces of democracy. Even when the blockade maintained by the Union navy cut off shipments of American cotton and starved the British textile industry, the unemployed spinners of Manchester remained loyal to the Northern states and the anti-slavery cause. Relations between Washington and London grew dangerously tense on several occasions, especially when warships built for the Confederacy in British shipyards were allowed to escape to sea. But the British cabinet resisted the suggestions of Napoleon III for joint Anglo-French intervention and preserved, though it did not always scrupulously enforce, the policy of neutrality towards both belligerents which it had proclaimed in May 1861.

The nationalistic fever that accompanied the struggles for Italian and German unity also had repercussions on British political life. Garibaldi received an enthusiastic popular reception during a visit to England in 1864. When the North German Confederation took form in 1866, with a Reichstag elected by equal, secret, direct manhood suffrage, the great English champion of parliamentary reform, John Bright, pointed out that in Great Britain the franchise was still denied to five men out of six. 'What is it that we are now come to in this country', he demanded, 'that what is being rapidly conceded in all parts of the world is being persistently and obstinately refused here in England, the home of freedom, the mother of Parliaments?' With Palmerston's death in 1865 the political reins were slackened, and Earl Russell, who succeeded him as prime minister, introduced a mild reform measure in 1866. But the bill was rejected, and a Conservative cabinet took office, headed by Lord Derby and Benjamin Disraeli. Popular agitation moved Disraeli to introduce a new bill designed to add 100,000 borough electors to the rolls, and he blandly accepted liberal amendments that quadrupled this number. Further clauses redistributed fifty-eight parliamentary seats, and the revised Bill was passed in 1867. Reform measures for Scotland and Ireland followed the next year, and the British people advanced another stride on the road to democracy. The number of electors almost doubled, for 2,448,000 possessed the franchise after this Second Reform Bill became law. Thenceforth not only the middle class but also a considerable portion of the working class were directly represented in the House of Commons.

The British Parliament did not legislate solely for the 31,000,000 inhabitants of the British Isles in 1867: it directed the destinies of an overseas empire of 200,000,000. Government at a distance, even when it is exercised with moderation and prudence, has inevitable defects. Of all the British imperial conquests, the vast subcontinent of India was the most profitable, complex, troubled, and vulnerable. British authority over the Indian states remained anomalous; some of them were independent allies of the Crown, some were vassals, some were annexed territories in which the administration had passed into the hands of British officials. After 1848 the vigorous administration of the Earl of Dalhousie (governor-general from 1848 to 1856) brought many improvements in public works, highways, railways, canals, bridges, irrigation schemes, telegraph and postal service. Dalhousie also sought to modify some of the more inhumane social and religious practices of India, notably suttee which Christian missionaries had denounced. Such administrative interference with time-honoured customs and the more resolute subordination of the Indian princes to British control, aroused a deepening resentment. During Dalhousie's term of office the Punjab, Oudh, and six lesser states were annexed; and the governor-general was criticized for this vigorous imperialism when he returned to England.

In 1857 a serious mutiny broke out in Bengal among the native Indian troops (sepoys). Within a few weeks it spread through the Ganges provinces and central India, threatening British control, but the rebellion lacked organization and capable leadership. The daring and energy of the small British garrisons available checked it by the end of the year with the aid of loyal Indian forces, and the rebels were punished with drastic severity. Most of the great princes had remained neutral, and the masses of India were scarcely stirred from their apathy. But the warning produced a change in British policy. The Mogul empire at Delhi was broken up; the Mogul was exiled and his sons put to death; and the proportion of British to Indian soldiers was heavily increased. The authority previously exercised by the British East India Company was transferred to the Crown under a new cabinet member, the secretary of state for India, and the governor-general became the viceroy. The programme of modernization, annexation, and missionary activity, which had helped to arouse the revolt, suffered a set-back, but British power in India was not materially reduced. On the contrary, the administrative officials learned much from the rebellion, and the Better Government of India Act (1858) helped to place British control on a more extensive and more adequate foundation.

Throughout eastern Asia the European powers, Britain, France, and Russia in particular, made significant gains in the period 1848–67. The British extended their influence in Burma while the French secured the three eastern provinces of Cochin China. Joint action by the two powers against China led to the occupation of the port of Canton (1858) and the sack of Peking (1860), the extortion of indemnities and trade concessions, and the legalization of the opium traffic. In the same years Russia induced the Chinese government to cede extensive areas east and west of the Amur river. In the Malayan archipelago the Dutch completed their subjugation of Bali (1849), extended their control in Java, and divided Timor and neighbouring islands with the Portuguese.

In the Americas the most critical development in the third quarter of the century was the civil war in the United States, the longest and costliest struggle that racked a great power between 1815 and 1914. For several decades before 1860 sectional differences between north and south had grown sharper. The northeastern states of the Union were dominated by commercial and industrial economy, while southern society remained essentially agrarian, with many large estates controlled by a planter aristocracy and worked by negro slaves. Successive attempts at a compromise on slavery, and especially on the problem of its extension to newly formed states in the west, failed to avert the 'irrepressible conflict', and the inauguration of Abraham Lincoln as president (4 March 1861) was followed by the secession of eleven southern states with a white population of 5,000,000. The advantages favouring the North indicated a swift decision, for the twenty-three states that remained in the Union had a population of 23,000,000 and contained the major financial, manufacturing, shipping, and railway resources of the nation. A blockade by Northern naval squadrons crippled the South by checking the export of cotton and the import of arms, and Union forces seized several coastal key points from Cape Hatteras to New Orleans. By 1863 the North had also secured control of the entire Mississippi valley, severing Texas, Arkansas, and Louisiana from the Confederacy. The Confederate armies fought brilliantly and desperately under the command of Robert E. Lee, who remained the outstanding military leader of the war, but Northern superiority in men and materials ultimately brought victory to the Union forces under General Ulysses S. Grant in the opening months of 1865.

On 14 April 1865 Abraham Lincoln was assassinated by a Southern fanatic shortly after his second inauguration. His stature as a statesman had grown steadily throughout the war years, and he was destined to take rank with Washington in the memory and affection of the American people. His rise from humble origins, his gaunt and homely appearance, his command of an English style that could range from uncouth frontier humour to a majestic biblical eloquence, the rare combination of compassion, shrewdness, faith, humility, and greatness in his character made Lincoln an enduring symbol of the democratic idea. He passed into history at the moment of victory, the Union saved, the slaves emancipated by his proclamation. His successor, Andrew Jackson, inherited the bitter and exacting problems of the Reconstruction era and had to cope with war-bred passions and prejudices while these were still unassuaged. Johnson's earliest act, after the capitulation of the last Confederate forces, was to proclaim a general amnesty for all ordinary persons involved in the rebellion (29 May 1865). Six months later, a thirteenth amendment was added to the Constitution, providing that 'Neither slavery nor involuntary servitude, except as a punishment for crime whereof the party shall have been duly convicted, shall exist within the United States, or any place subject to their jurisdiction.'

The American Civil War was the first major conflict in which railways helped to decide the outcome and mechanized industry revealed its startling potentialities for war production. European military observers learned important lessons on the effect of rifled artillery (which rendered many existing forts obsolete), on the importance of sea power and naval blockade, and on the colossal problems of transport and supply that had to be solved when nearly a million men were placed under arms. The cost of the war in men and money also provided grim warnings, for the total casualties on both sides reached almost half a million; the federal debt increased forty-fold in four years; and the Southern states were left devastated and prostrate by defeat, with the bonds and currency of the Confederacy reduced to worthless paper.

It was a curious comment on the partiality of most European observers that they ignored almost completely a second and more lethal war that ravaged another American republic in the 1860's. The militaristic state of Paraguay, a nation of over a million people ruled by the ambitious dictator, Francisco Solano Lôpez, took up arms against Brazil, Argentina, and Uruguay in 1865. The resulting five years' struggle virtually annihilated the Paraguayan people. Though exact figures are unavailable, it is probable that the toll from battles, reprisals, disease, and starvation reached three-quarters of a million dead. By 1870 estimates placed the surviving Paraguayans at 28,000 men and 200,000 women, a disproportion of one to seven. The republic, stripped of manpower, wealth, and half its territory, never recovered from its staggering losses in the War of the Allies.

Throughout the greater part of Latin America the decades after 1850 continued the familiar record of border disputes, civil wars, and military coups. The problems of centralization versus federalism, dictatorship versus parliamentarianism, clericalism versus secularism, and peons versus landlords, found no stable or enduring solutions. The most nearly tranquil states were the empire of Brazil, where a scion of the Portuguese royal house, Pedro II, maintained order throughout a long reign (1831–89), and Chile, where democracy made moderate progress under liberal presidents.

The history of Mexico in these years included one brief and tragic chapter, influenced in part by the contemporary civil war in the United States. The picturesque dictator, Antonio López de Santa Anna, was swept aside by a group of liberal reformers in 1855, and a remarkably able organizer of Indian blood, Benito Juarez, assumed leadership. For three years (1858–61) Juarez waged the War of the Reform, aiming at the secularization of Church property, reduction of military privileges, and improvement in the condition of the peons. He was elected president of the republic in 1861; but his repudiation of foreign loans and investments led to intervention by a European power, which judged it safe to ignore the Monroe Doctrine while the United States was weakened by civil conflict. Napoleon III dispatched a military force, predominantly French, which entered Mexico City and set up an empire (1864–7) under a Habsburg archduke who assumed the title Maximilian I, Emperor of Mexico. With the collapse of the Confederate cause in 1865, the State Department at Washington insisted that the United States would not recognize Maximilian and demanded the withdrawal of foreign troops from Mexico. Napoleon III was alarmed by events in Europe (the Austro-Prussian War impended) and disappointed at Maximilian's failure to liquidate the thousand-million-franc debt owed by the insolvent Mexican treasury. Accordingly, French forces were recalled in 1866; Maximilian remained to be captured and shot (19 June 1867); and Juarez returned to power. This outcome proved that the United States was prepared to enforce the Monroe Doctrine, brought discredit upon the French, and left Mexico with the perennial problems of the Church question, the land question, militarism, and foreign debts still unsolved.

Like the Mexicans, the people of the Canadian provinces felt the indirect repercussions of the American Civil War. Canadian export trade to the United States rose rapidly during the years 1861–5, stimulated by war demands and by a reciprocity agreement previously concluded in 1854. When the United States abrogated this treaty in 1866, the dislocation of their economy threw the Canadians back upon their own market. They were also disturbed by the Russian cession of Alaska to the United States (1867), by the military power of their southern neighbour, and by Irish-American groups (Fenians) who raided some Canadian border towns to bring pressure to bear upon the British Parliament to free Ireland. Realizing that a common policy among their scattered provinces would provide the best answer to the problems of defence, economic development, internal communication, and immigration, the Canadians decided to establish a federal

government, and the Dominion of Canada was created
by the British North America Act passed by the British
Parliament in 1867. The promise that railway con-
nexions would be established helped to draw in the
outlying provinces; Novia Scotia and New Brunswick
joined in 1867, Manitoba in 1870, and British Columbia
in 1869. The government of the new Dominion of
Canada consisted of a senate and a lower house with a
governor-general to represent the British Crown.
Canada thus took its place as the first self-governing
dominion in the British Commonwealth, a new nation
of more than 3,000,000 people, with an area (still partly
unexplored) that was later estimated at 3,000,000
square miles.

Throughout the years 1848–67, in the Americas as
in Europe, the impulse towards nation-building
appeared and reappeared as the dominant political
trend of the period. From the Hungarian revolt to the
Paraguayan holocaust the most sanguinary struggles
were an expression of this desire to found or to expand
a nation state. Russian expansion in the Near East
produced the Crimean War of 1854–6; the spirit of the
risorgimento ignited the Italian War of 1859; national
aspirations roused the Poles to revolt in 1863; the desire
of the Danish monarchs to consolidate their realm
provoked the Danish War of 1864; Prussian plans for
the unification of the Germanies precipitated the Austro-
Prussian War of 1866. The exasperation that drove the
people of the southern section to secede from the
United States in 1861 proved less powerful than the
will of the majority of the nation to preserve the Union.

Whether the demands for independence and expansion were frustrated by superior forces, as in the case of the Hungarians, the Russians, the Poles, the Confederate states, and the Paraguayan republic, or whether the will to unity triumphed, as in Italy, Germany, the United States, and Canada, this desire to forge or to preserve the nation state revealed itself as the most powerful and imperious impulse agitating the western world.

The second political principle that shaped the age, the principle of parliamentary democracy, advanced more hesitantly and within narrower confines. In Great Britain it made substantial progress; in Italy, the North German Confederation, and the Austrian empire representative government won a varying measure of recognition; in the Netherlands, Denmark, Sweden Switzerland, and Greece, constitutional reforms curtailed the prerogatives of the rulers and increased the powers of the popular chambers. But in France the democratic republic of 1848 was transformed into a virtual dictatorship by 1852; and in Russia the autocratic régime was only slightly softened by the concessions of Alexander II. The two outstanding reforms of this era, reforms that altered the legal status of more than 50,000,000 human beings, were the emancipation of 47,000,000 Russian serfs and more than 5,000,000 American negro slaves. These were notable triumphs for which the growth of humanitarian sentiment had prepared the way. Slavery was abolished in the British colonies in 1833, in the French in 1848, in the Netherlands East Indies after 1863, and in the Portuguese possessions between 1858 and 1878. Latin American governments anticipated or followed the European example, Colombia by stages after 1821, Mexico (1829), Argentina (1853), Venezuela (1854), Peru (1856), and Brazil (1871–88).

The progress of western technology in the period 1848–67 was marked by significant improvements in communication, metallurgy, and military weapons, a fitting anvil chorus to an age punctuated by such frequent and expensive wars. Railway and telegraph lines branched out rapidly. The first electric submarine telegraph was laid from Dover to Calais in 1851; six years later a transatlantic cable was completed, but a permanent service was not established until 1866. Urgent demands for better and cheaper steel and gun metal led Henry Bessemer to develop a method for decarbonizing molten pig-iron with an oxidizing blast (1856). Ten years later the regenerative gas furnace, improved by William Siemens in England and Pierre Martin in France, extended the use of the open-hearth process and inaugurated a veritable age of steel. The first ironclad warship was built for Napoleon III in 1859, and the civil war in the United States provided the first effective test of naval armour-plate in the historic duel of the U.S.S. *Monitor* and the C.S.S. *Merrimac* on 9 March 1862. Improvements in weapons included the rifling of artillery and small arms (1855), and the invention of the repeating rifle (1860), the machine-gun (1862), and the first efficient locomotive torpedo (1866).

In the intellectual world the most momentous event of the age was the publication of Charles Darwin's classic study, *On the Origin of Species by Means of Natural Selection*, in 1859. Darwin's theory reinforced the naturalistic currents in contemporary thought and was destined to influence not only the scientific, but also the social, historical, philosophical, and religious speculations of the following generation. But a theory that related man biologically to the anthropoid apes was too repugnant and too revolutionary to win rapid acceptance, and the vast majority of people in England and elsewhere shared Disraeli's reaction when he declared in 1864:

What is the question now placed before society with the glib assurance which to me is most astonishing? That question is this: Is man an ape or an angel? I, my lord, am on the side of the angels. I repudiate with indignation and abhorrence those new-fangled theories.

Chapter Four

SCIENTIFIC MATERIALISM AND 'REALPOLITIK' (1867–81)

THE forging of Italy and Germany into nation states altered the map of Europe and shifted the balance of power. Falling almost midway between 1815 and 1914 this climax of nation building separated the nineteenth century into two halves, with the year 1867 as an approximate watershed dividing the new Europe from the old. But political and military crises were not the only evidence of a significant demarcation. There were profounder trends, less sudden and dramatic but more fateful, steadily transforming the European inheritance, and they gained momentum when the flurry of the mid-century wars had passed.

At first glance the later half of the nineteenth century seems to differ so sharply from the earlier that the contrasts are more significant than the continuities. By 1867 the national centralized territorial state had become the triumphant political scheme of the age; the older federal ideal was largely discredited; and the Concert of Europe had retreated into the limbo reserved for diplomatic fictions. A technological revolution was remoulding the economic foundations of European and North American society. Industry superseded agriculture as the major economic activity of the western world, and town dwellers came to outnumber and outvote the rural population. The new industrialism gave impulsion to a new imperialism, and factory production created the wares and the weapons that enabled great powers to compete for the trade of a shrinking planet. On all levels of western society the rising material prosperity was the accepted yardstick of progress, and the thought of the age yielded to the dogmas of scientific materialism and *Realpolitik*. The prestige of the priests and the philosophers dimmed before that of the scientists, and the unsubstantial pageant of the romantic sunset was followed by the cold dawn of positivist philosophy and realistic art.

In the fourteen years between 1867 and 1881 this new Europe hardened into the definitive political matrix it was to retain until the First World War. The salient fact in the new international pattern was the ascendancy of Germany. Throughout the first half of the nineteenth century four great powers, Austria, Russia, Prussia, and France, had dominated the Continent, while Britain stood apart; but after 1867 this quadrilateral balance of power was a thing of the past. The political unification of Italy (1859–61) added a new state which counted (in area and population at least) as a fifth great power, and the creation of the North German Confederation (1867) doubled the strength and influence of Prussia. For France the consolidation of Italy and Germany involved an ominous risk, because it meant that thenceforth two first-class powers would be wedged against the French frontiers where previously there had been only divided secondary states. The formation of the North German Confederation shifted the diplomatic and military centre of Europe from Paris to Berlin, and those who failed to read this lesson aright had it thrust upon their attention promptly in a dramatic and terrible fashion.

In the summer of 1870 the Spanish Cortes invited a German prince, Leopold of Hohenzollern-Sigmaringen, to mount the throne at Madrid. Two years earlier a liberal insurrection had driven out the incapable Isabella II and opened a period of experiment and instability in Spain which was not to end until Isabella's son assumed the crown in 1875 as Alphonso XII. The invitation to Leopold was a makeshift expedient, but when news of it reached Paris in July 1870, it excited profound dissatisfaction there. The counsellors who surrounded Napoleon III foresaw a Prusso-Spanish alliance, and the French ambassador to Berlin, Vincente Benedetti, was instructed to insist that Leopold should decline the proferred crown. This was arranged, but the accommodation failed to placate French resentment. Benedetti in an interview pressed William I for further guarantees and apologies, but without success. Bismarck published an account of the interview in brusque phrases (the Ems telegram) that sharpened the antagonism on both sides, and the French council of ministers decided that Prussia must be humiliated even if it meant war. Relying upon unfounded assurances of Austrian and Italian aid the chambers supported a declaration of hostilities (19 July) while the Parisian crowds shouted 'On to Berlin'.

The Franco-Prussian War lasted six months and proved a shattering defeat for the French. No help came from Italy; the government of Victor Emmanuel seized the opportunity created by the withdrawal of French troops at Rome to occupy the Eternal City. The Austrians waited (as the French had done in 1866) until the chance for effective intervention had passed. The Russian court preserved a benevolent neutrality towards Prussia, and welcomed the diversion created by the discomfiture of France because it permitted Russia to throw off the restrictions inposed by the treaty of Paris fourteen years earlier and to refortify the Black Sea bases. In London the Liberal cabinet headed by Gladstone was satisfied with promises from France and Prussia that the neutrality of Belgium would be respected. Bismarck published the injudicious demands for Belgian or Rhineland territory that Napoleon had pressed in 1866, a revelation that weakened any British sympathy towards France and rallied the south as well as the north German states to the Prussian cause. By 2 September 1870 Napoleon was forced to capitulate at Sedan with 100,000 men, while a second French army of 173,000 under Marshal Bazaine surrendered at Metz on 27 October.

The news of Sedan overthrew the Second Empire. In Paris Republican leaders, headed by the energetic Léon Gambetta, proclaimed a Government of National Defence. But the war was already lost, and heroic efforts to raise new French armies prolonged the fighting without reversing the decision. German forces surrounded Paris and starvation forced the city to surrender on 28 January 1871. Two weeks later a newly elected French National Assembly met at Bordeaux and voted for peace. By the treaty of Frankfurt (10 May 1871) France ceded Alsace and part of Lorraine, and pledged herself to pay an indemnity of 5,000,000,000 francs.

The tragic events of 'the terrible year' were not yet over. Radical leaders in Paris denounced the 'reactionary' Assembly that had made a humiliating peace, and the Parisian National Guard refused to surrender its arms. The assembly, which had moved to Versailles, decided to subdue the rebellious capital, and Adolphe Thiers, elected Chief of the Executive Power, pressed the attack while the German victors looked on. There was no unity of aim or of command among the Paris Comunards, and their resistance was broken after weeks of bloody fighting that ended in blind massacre and reprisal. By June Thiers had restored order in Paris at a cost of 10,000 to 20,000 lives.

The Third French Republic, born in an hour of national defeat, survived almost by chance the vicissitudes of its early period. For five years the assembly hastily elected in 1871 clung to power; a majority of the members were monarchists, but they failed to unite behind a Legitimist, Orleanist, or Bonapartist pretender, and a general election in 1876 gave the republicans a majority in the Chamber of Deputies. Three years later they won control in the Senate also. Marshal MacMahon (who had replaced Thiers in 1873) resigned, and the national representatives chose a safe republican, Jules Grévy, to succeed him. By 1879, therefore, the Third French Republic had been consolidated as a moderately stable bourgeois régime. It was destined to survive until 1940, the most durable government the French people had known since the collapse of the ancient monarchy in the Revolution of 1789.

The Franco-Prussian War, which made France a republic, made Germany an empire. Leading German princes acclaimed William I of Prussia German emperor in the palace of Louis XIV at Versailles (18 January 1871) while the guns of Paris, a few miles away, were firing their last despairing volleys. Bismarck had rightly calculated that a common victory over an ancient foe would fuse the German nation. In structure, the new empire was an extension of the North German Confederation of 1867, with the four south German states (Bavaria, Würtemberg, Baden and, Hesse–Darmstadt) added. The imperial Bundesrat and Reichstag sat in Berlin, and Bismarck maintained his position as chancellor of the new Reich. His prestige was now almost unassailable. Under his leadership Prussia had won three wars in seven years, ended Danish, Austrian, and French interference in German affairs, and created a German empire of 41,000,000 people, the most powerful military state in Europe.

After 1871 Bismarck turned his chief attention to internal politics, labouring to consolidate the empire he had shaped. For eight years he waged a contest with the German Catholics because he believed it essential to reduce the influence of the Catholic orders and clergy, expecially in education. But persecution failed in its purpose, and the Centre party, through which the Catholics defended their political and religious influence, grew stronger under attack. Meanwhile socialism was also gaining ground, until by 1878 Bismarck saw it as a greater threat than Catholicism. He therefore eased his struggle (*Kulturkampf*) against the Catholic Church, opened negotiations with the new Pope, Leo XIII, and invited support from the Centre party. He had decided to embark on a radical change of policy.

While he was forging the empire Bismarck had leaned upon the National Liberals, and he found the middle-class business men and the professional groups loyal in their support. The National Liberals favoured German unity, but they also demanded free speech, a free press, free trade, and responsible parliamentary government. When Bismarck broke with them after 1878, he swung back to the conservative position more natural to him; he curbed the press, repressed the Socialists, and adopted a protective tariff. This reversal pleased the Prussian landowners and the great industrialists, but it 'turned the clock back' and split the National Liberal forces. By 1879 the new German Reich stood revealed as a militant, industrialized, authoritarian state in which powerful conservative groups would control the régime behind a façade of representative government. In France, almost at the same moment, the Third Republic took definitive form as a parliamentary bourgeois democracy in which the executive power and the conservative groups (Catholics, monarchists, militarists) were to be held in check and subordinated to the rule of parliament. Thus from St. Petersburg to Paris the political spectrum of Europe shaded from autocracy to parliamentarianism, preserving the gradations that had distinguished it since the Congress of Vienna.

In Great Britain the election of 1868 swept the Liberals into power under William Ewart Gladstone. This devout and humanitarian statesman dedicated his first ministry to domestic problems, to the reform of education, of the judicature, and of the army. But the issue nearest his heart was the ancient and envenomed Irish Question. 'My mission', he announced, 'is to pacify Ireland', and he laboured at it, in and out of office, for thirty years. The grievances the Irish nursed against England had a threefold root: religious, economic, and political. In 1869 Gladstone disestablished the (Episcopal) Church of Ireland, freeing Irish Catholics from the compulsion to support a church they did not attend. In 1870 an Irish Land Act improved the lot of the Irish tenantry, but it failed to provide the fair rent, fixity of tenure, and free sale demanded by the Tenant-Right League. Irish agitation and agrarian violence persisted, and the resentment of Irish landlords and Anglican clergy stayed the hope of further reforms. In 1874 the Conservatives carried the elections.

As Tory prime minister for the following six years Benjamin Disraeli dazzled the British public with a foreign policy reminiscent of the Palmerstonian era. His purchase of Suez Canal shares from the Khedive of Egypt (1875) gave Britain partial control of that vital waterway which had been completed in 1869 through French initiative. In 1876 an Act declared Queen Victoria 'Empress of India', and the flattered sovereign made Disraeli Earl of Beaconsfield. But the resumption of imperialism carried its risks and penalties. In Egypt Britain and France assumed joint responsibility for straightening out the Khedive's finances; but the condominium ended with Britain in charge. In 1877 the British annexed the South African Republic (in breach of an earlier understanding with the Dutch settlers) and provoked a revolt of the Transvaal Boers, complicated by local wars with the Kaffirs and Zulus. In India a Second Afghan War broke out in 1878. These, however, were distant and peripheral threats. The real crisis in foreign affairs during Disraeli's second ministry was the revival of Anglo-Russian tension over the Near Eastern question. It brought the two powers as close to war as they could come and still avoid it.

A free outlet to the Mediterranean Sea or the Indian Ocean was a logical goal of Russian imperialism, but it meant the subjugation of Turkey or Persia. By 1870 all the signs indicated that Russian ambitions for conquest were reviving. The restrictions imposed after the Crimean War were repudiated, internal reforms languished, and Alexander's officials turned to reorganize the army and expand the programme of military training. The Balkans were seething; insurrections against Turkish misrule broke out in Herzegovina and Bosnia in 1875, spread to Serbia, and were followed by an uprising in Bulgaria (1876) which was repressed in murderous fashion by the Turkish irregulars (the 'Bulgarian Atrocities'). Russia could no longer be restrained, and by 1877 the Tsar's forces were fighting their way towards Constantinople, where the British Mediterranean fleet cast anchor in February 1878 to forestall them. Once again the Russians had overreached themselves, for the terms they exacted from the Turks were rejected by Britain and Austria. With deep reluctance Alexander II agreed to refer the entire Balkan question to a general international conference.

The Congress of Berlin of 1878 was the most notable diplomatic assembly since that of Vienna sixty-three years earlier. All six European great powers were represented, and the settlement was a typical example of reciprocal compensation. Russia kept southern Bessarabia, Batum, Kars, and Ardahan. Austria received a mandate to occupy Bosnia and Herzegovina. Britain occupied Cyprus. Greece obtained Thessaly, and Bulgaria was left partly autonomous and partly tributary. Serbia, Rumania, and Montenegro became independent. The French (not yet recovered from their defeat in 1870) were put off with a promise of Tunis, and the Italians with vaguer promises respecting Albania. Disraeli and Salisbury returned from Berlin with the announcement that they had achieved peace with honour, but subsequent developments threw doubt on their statesmanship. In extending Austrian influence in the Balkans they had prepared the way for an Austro-German *Drang nach Osten*. But no premonition of this future peril dimmed the jingoistic mood of the British public in July of 1878. It was Disraeli's hour, all the sweeter because the Russians were bitter with frustration.

At St. Petersburg deep official resentment over the Berlin settlement was reflected in the press, but it was directed, somewhat illogically, against Bismarck rather than Disraeli. The Russians felt themselves the dupes of their neighbours' ingratitude. They had aided the Habsburg monarchy in 1849, yet Austria had favoured

France and Britain in the Crimean War; they had adopted a benevolent neutrality towards Prussia in 1870–1, yet at the Congress of Berlin Bismarck had looked on while they were robbed of their Turkish conquests. It seemed a shabby return for so much altruism, and Alexander II wrote a heated rebuke to William I. Bismarck hoped the Russian indignation would burn itself out, but he wasted no time on explanations or regrets. Turning to Vienna he arranged an Austro-German Alliance (1879) that was in substance a defensive pact against Russia or France or both. Then, after relations between Berlin and St. Petersburg improved again, the eastern powers reaffirmed their earlier friendship, and Prussia, Austria, and Russia concluded a secret accord suitably known as the Three Emperors' League (1881). If any one of the partners became involved in war with a fourth power (Turkey excepted) the other two promised friendly neutrality. The Three Emperors' League was renewable every third year; it lapsed within the decade; and its chief interest is the clue it provides to Bismarck's 'nightmare of coalitions' that might be formed against Germany. He would have neutralized Britain by similar diplomacy if he could. In 1882 he did succeed in drawing Italy into the Austro-German agreement, transforming the Dual into a Triple Alliance. For Germany the value of this elaborate and negative Bismarckian System was that it left France isolated. If the French chauvinists undertook a war of revenge to reconquer Alsace–Lorraine they would have to fight it alone.

For two decades after 1878 international tensions in

Europe tended to relax. This easing of the pressures
nearer home left the great powers more freedom of
action overseas, and the last twenty years of the nineteenth century found them competing more keenly for
unclaimed areas of Africa and Asia. After 1900, when
almost all Africa and the more vulnerable portions of
Asia had been pre-empted, the international pressure
in Europe mounted once more. These developments
will be discussed more fully in a later chapter.

Across the Atlantic the United States, like the leading
European powers, took on its modern aspect in the
decades after 1865. The war between the states had
given machine industry an extraordinary impetus and
speeded up the construction of railway and telegraph
lines. The first transcontinental railway from the
Atlantic to the Pacific was completed in 1869; three
more followed within twenty years. By 1876 refrigerator
cars were rushing chilled meat from Kansas City to
New York, whence refrigerated ships carried it to
Europe. Barbed wire conquered the Great Plains,
separating herds and guarding grain lands, and chilled
steel rollers were invented to mill the mounting wheat
crops. The integration of the American economy, and
its expansion to match the margins of a continental
market, provided the most dynamic development of the
Reconstruction era: American 'Big Business' leaped
from its cradle with steel sinews and a giant's appetite.
High wages encouraged the introduction of machinery;
there was a shortage of manpower although the population was rising at an unprecedented rate. By 1880 the
American nation had passed 50,000,000 outstripping

in population every great power of that day except Russia.

This phenomenal American business prosperity threw a strain on democratic institutions that bent and almost broke them. Western farmers were angered by the unfair monopolistic practices of railways and flour-mills, and sought vainly for legislation to bring them under control. State legislatures were suborned by bribery, and the administration of President Grant was disfigured by revelations of corruption that forced Congressmen from office and drove members of the cabinet to resign. Inflation and over-expansion finally took their toll, and in 1873 a panic shook the financial centres of the United States and Europe, reflecting (as the earlier panic of 1857 had done) the increasing interdependence of the international economy. But the resiliency of American business enterprise was proved by its vigorous recovery. Europe needed the agricultural products of the New World, gold flowed to the United States, business confidence returned, and in 1879 the Treasury resumed specie payments.

To the Dominion of Canada, unified by the Act of Confederation of 1867, the subsequent decade brought no radical changes. Discontent among the half-breeds of Manitoba excited them to a brief rebellion, easily repressed (1869–70). Projects for a transcontinental railway were bogged down in political scandals until a new charter organized the Canadian Pacific Railway Company and the line was completed in 1885. As in the United States the population shifted westward and increased steadily, reaching 4,324,810 by 1881.

To the Latin American peoples the period brought one notable conflict, the War of the Pacific (1879–83), in which Chile defeated Peru and Bolivia, emerging as the dominant power of the Andean region. A ten-year revolt in Cuba (which had remained under the Spanish Crown) ended in 1878 with promises of reform from Madrid that were not kept. The United States, which had sought to purchase the island earlier, did not intervene; and when the people of Haiti invited annexation (1870) the United States Senate showed equal restraint by rejecting the proposal. More surprising was the negative attitude in Washington in 1878, when the republic of Columbia granted a French company (headed by Ferdinand de Lesseps) a ninety-nine-year lease with exclusive rights to build an inter-oceanic canal across the isthmus of Panama. Not until twenty years later, after De Lesseps's company had foundered, and plans for an alternative Nicaraguan canal had miscarried, did the United States government undertake the Panama venture in a conviction that 'manifest destiny' prescribed it.

American initiative lagged in cutting the isthmus because the people of the United States were slow to recognize their nation as a power in the Pacific. The westward movement was so swift that it outstripped calculation. In the west coast states (Washington, Oregon, and California) the population multiplied tenfold in thirty years; by 1880 it was well over one million. American pressure, naval and commercial, had begun to influence the ancient empires of east Asia for a generation before the American people were awake to this new responsibility. The part played by the United

States navy in the awakening of Japan was a striking illustration of this absent-minded imperialism.

Proud, feudal, and self-sufficient, the Japanese people had rejected contacts with Europeans since the expulsion of Christian missionaries early in the seventeenth century. Save for a single restricted Dutch trading post at Nagasaki, Japan remained isolated from the rest of the world until the middle of the nineteenth century; but then the policy of exclusion was abandoned with startling results. In 1853 and 1854 American warships visited Edo Bay, and Commodore Matthew Calbraith Perry extorted a treaty that opened two Japanese ports to American trade. Britain, Russia and the Netherlands promptly secured similar privileges, and the Japanese ruling nobility was split over the question of accepting or rejecting foreign intercourse. Western technological supremacy decided the issue; in 1864 an allied expedition of British, French, Dutch, and American frigates shelled the Japanese defences at Shimonoseki; and in 1865 the four powers secured broader trade conventions. The demonstration of western weapons and their irresistible effect wrought a revolution in Japanese thought and politics.

For generations the authority of the Japanese emperor (Mikado) had been eclipsed by that of the Shogun, a hereditary official with extraordinary powers. In 1868 a young, capable, and realistic emperor, Mutsuhito (1867–1912), reasserted the imperial dignity, moved his capital to Tokyo, and opened a new period in Japanese history. The Shogun resigned, the feudal warlords surrendered their semi-independent powers, and the xenophobia of the preceding period was officially abandoned. Instead of rejecting all things occidental, the statesmen of the new régime imitated and adopted western institutions. The Japanese navy was remodelled on that of Great Britain; the army leaders studied and incorporated Prussian methods; the educators borrowed American practices. Japanese law courts and codes introduced French and German procedures; new legislation was approved in constitutional fashion by an elected diet and chamber of peers comparable to European parliaments. No less remarkable was the rapid reorganization of Japanese industry. Students travelled abroad to observe and master western business methods, and returned to plan railways, shipyards, factories, banks, hotels, department stores, and newspapers in their homeland. Seldom in history had a nation devoted itself to such sedulous imitation since the Japanese themselves adopted Chinese culture and customs fifteen centuries earlier. Europeans observed the furious awakening of the island kingdom with an amused tolerance, and Arthur Sullivan and W. S. Gilbert, in their light opera *The Mikado* (1885), created a mythical picture of Japan that was a source of innocent merriment. The awakening of Europe to the real significance of the Japanese revolution was to come later.

The outstanding characteristic that the Japanese borrowed from Europe, and the problem which the nineteenth century posed for the twentieth century to answer, was that of a runaway technology. The age of steam and steel, of a coal economy and machine production, achieved its first centenary in the western world around 1870. The preceding century had seen a stable agricultural and commercial society transformed by the dynamics of industrialism. The designation 'Industrial Revolution' frequently applied to this social and economic transformation is far from satisfactory, though it had persisted for want of a more exact designation. The central fact in the rise of nineteenth-century industry was not the invention of machinery (machines of exceptional ingenuity and flexibility had been perfected earlier), but the application of a cheap and plentiful source of power for driving the machines. One pound of coal, when efficiently burned, yielded more energy than a human being expended in a day's work, and the steam-engine was a more dependable servant than the older machines run by wind, water, or animal power. The classic example of the expansion that might be wrought by power-driven machinery was the revolution in the British textile industry. In the decade 1810–20 this industry provided employment for 250,000 workers, but only one in twenty-five laboured in a factory. Sixty years later the number of workers was approximately the same, but all had by then abandoned home looms for factory labour. The social and environmental revolution that overtook these textile workers and their dependents had, inevitably, produced significant and often adverse changes in their mode of life. But this was not the most arresting fact in the transition to machine production. The consideration which brought about the change to the factory system was the fact that it increased the output per worker

K

twelvefold. By 1880 the same number of textile hands (approximately 250,000), using power-driven machinery, were turning out as much fabric as 3,000,000 workers could have produced under the domestic system.

That modern machine industry was built on coal was testified by the rate of its consumption. Between 1670 and 1770 the annual European coal production increased only threefold. Between 1770 and 1870 (the century of the Industrial Revolution) it rose thirtyfold. But this first century of industrialism, impressive and even revolutionary though its effects proved, was only a prologue. After 1870 (until European economy was dislocated by the First World War) the average increase in coal production *each decade* was greater than the total increase for the preceding century. After 1870, therefore, it became increasingly evident that western civilization was geared to a runaway technology.

Such a spurt in the progress of industrialism, after the movement had been steadily accelerating for a hundred years, indicates that after 1870 western economy entered a new phase, a 'New Industrial Revolution'. There was unquestionably a quickening of the tempo, a broadening of research, a constellation of inventions that made the 1870's a decade of unparalleled expansion. Before it closed scientists and engineers had begun to challenge the reign of King Coal by demonstrating the commercial possibilities of two alternative sources of energy. By 1881 the production of petroleum already exceed 3,000,000 tons annually, and the oil industry had been born. More significant still, newly perfected dynamos in electric power plants were generating current for light circuits and other commercial purposes. The age of oil and electricity was at hand, with its incredible instruments of power and precision, waiting to transform the living standards of the western world. The dawning era could not fail to be an age of industry, but it proved to be much more than that. The rapid increase in human powers and potentialities that dazzled western man in the last quarter of the nineteenth century was more than a second industrial revolution. It would be more accurate to say that the new era brought a technological revolution, and to call the period that opened about 1870 the technological age.

The new instruments of power and precision that appeared in the early years of this technological era read like a catalogue of scientific marvels. Between 1867 and 1881 the telephone, microphone, electric lamp, gramophone, internal combustion engine, and electric tram-car made their first appearance. Advances in dry-plate photography, elementary colour photography, and motion pictures opened new avenues of research. The rotary perfecting press and the typewriter speeded labour in printing shop and office. Nor was mechanization confined to industry. The improved reaper and binder enabled the farmer to expand his acres while chemical fertilizers increased the yield. Transportation costs fell while the speed and regularity of the carriers improved; the airbrake solved the problem of deceleration; and railroad tunnels through the Alps (Mont Cenis, 1871; Saint Gothard, 1882) reduced

the journey from Italy to Germany or France from days
to hours. The Suez Canal, which enabled vessels to
pass from the Mediterranean to the Red Sea and Indian
Ocean, and the first transcontinental railway to cross
the United States, were both opened in the same year
(1869).

Man's growing mastery over his physical environment, his victories over time and space, were matched
in this period by his discoveries about himself. Charles
Darwin's treatises *On the Origin of Species by Means of
Natural Selection* (1859) and *The Descent of Man* (1871)
gave a profound impulse to the study of biology and
anthropology. Gregor Mendel's researches into the
mechanics of heredity (1865) were overlooked for a
generation, but Francis Galton emphasized the role of
inheritance in the mental development of human beings
(1867), and Wilhelm Wundt demonstrated the interdependence of mind and body in his *Principles of
Physiological Psychology* (1872). The concept of evolution and the principle of natural selection were applied
to human customs and institutions by Walter Bagehot
(1873). Interest in the new theories concerning man's
origin and development spread rapidly among scientifi-
cally inclined laymen and were popularized by forceful
writers and lecturers such as Thomas Henry Huxley in
England and Ernest Haeckel in Germany.

Nothing brought the scientists more prestige than
advances in medicine and surgery: people in every
station were fascinated by the report of new victories
over pain, disease, and death. Antiseptic surgery, introduced by Joseph Lister (1865), directed attention to the

importance of bacteria as agents of infection. Louis Pasteur and Robert Koch gave a shrewd blow to the immemorial belief in spontaneous generation by proving that germs were not merely the concomitants but the cause of great plagues. Within half-a-dozen years the bacteriologists, working with tireless zeal, identified the bacillus of leprosy, the malaria parasite, the bacteria of anthrax, and the germs of tuberculosis, diphtheria, and Asiatic cholera. A dramatic inoculation by Pasteur (1885) saved the life of a boy who had been bitten by a mad dog and marked the first sure step in the conquest of hydrophobia. Physicians could now recognize the enemies that hitherto they had fought in the dark, and could safeguard possible victims of many deadly diseases by the administration of serums and antitoxins. A new branch of medicine had come into being, the science of immunology.

Every hypothesis of the scientists, when vindicated by experiment, advertised the efficacy of their methods and invested the positivist approach with greater authority. Chemists and biologists, physicists and geologists did not stop to ponder (as the speculative philosophers had so often done) imponderable essences and unverifiable generalities; they handled the stuff of life and the building blocks of matter. When Dmitri Mendeleeff first published his Periodic Law of the Elements (1869), arguing that they would be found, when ranged according to their atomic weights, to display a certain periodicity, so that each eighth element revealed somewhat similar properties, his table won attention as a further proof that nature was intelligible to those who accepted her pronouncements. A strong conviction had grown up that everything in the physical universe was behaving in a rational manner and that it was man's disorderly mind that had led him to misread her. The major obstacle to the progress of science, many rationalists insisted, was the heritage of conceit and superstition that induced men to prefer a flattering illusion to an unflattering truth. The march of scientific discovery had been achieved through the depersonalization of myths. Among the myths that would ultimately be discredited, or so some agnostics proclaimed, were many articles of the Christian faith, especially those that involved a belief in miraculous events and appeared to contradict natural laws and the natural order.

This growing conflict between rationalism and religion, between the scientist and the theologian, was sharpened by the controversy over the Darwinian theory of biological evolution. Fundamentally, however, the dispute was deeper and more ancient. It was the recurrent argument between the materialist, who believes that the facts of the universe can be sufficiently explained by the existence and nature of matter, and the transcendentalist who asserts the primacy of spiritual over empirical truth. In 1864 Pope Pius IX issued a famous encyclical, *Quanta cura*, and in an accompanying syllabus he warned the faithful against 'the principal errors of our time'. It was not true, the syllabus emphasized, that God did not exist, or that all action by God upon man and upon the world was to be denied. Nor was it true that human reason, without any

regard to God, was the sole arbiter of truth or false-
hood, or that the miracles narrated in the Holy Scriptures were poetic fictions and the Testaments contained
mythical inventions.

Had the papal warning paused with this condemnation of philosophical materialism and agnosticism it
might have excited less comment, but Pius went on to
rebuke those anticlericals and nationalists who insisted
upon the supremacy of the secular State, and those
liberals who favoured the separation of Church and
state and advocated the establishment of secular education. The final clause of the syllabus (number 80)
specifically rejected the idea that the Roman Pontiff
could or should reconcile himself with progress,
liberalism, or modern civilization, and this declaration
seemed to many to set the Roman Church squarely
athwart the intellectual and political currents of the
age. Although the syllabus of errors was not proclaimed
as dogma, and leading Catholic apologists hastened to
explain that it should be considered as an admonition
evoked in part by contemporary developments in Italy,
it aroused a sharp debate on the nature and extent of the
papal authority. The dispute was not softened but
intensified when the Vatican Council defined the dogma
of papal infallibility (1870). This twentieth oecumenical
council of the Roman Catholic Church (the first
general council since the sixteenth century) declared it
to be a dogma 'divinely revealed' that the Roman Pontiff,
when he spoke *ex cathedra*, possessed 'that infallibility
with which the Divine Redeemer willed that His
Church should be endowed for defining faith and

morals'. This proclamation marked the high point in
the pontificate of Pius IX. Before the close of 1870 the
forces of the new Italian kingdom had occupied Rome,
the council had adjourned, and Pius was 'the prisoner
of the Vatican'. In Great Britain, France, and especially
in Germany, criticism of the papal claims was acute and
prolonged. A liberal group in the German empire who
became known as the Old Catholics, refused to be
bound by the decision of the council, and Bismarck
supported their revolt, opening a struggle between state
and Church in Germany (the *Kulturkampf*) that lasted
throughout the 1870's.

A widening rift divided those who accepted religious
dogmas as literal, unchanging truths and those who admitted that all the great prophets, including Jesus, had
been influenced by the social and intellectual conditions
of their environment. Biblical scholars who came to
feel that the Old and New Testaments should be
evaluated by the same methods that historians used to
determine the credibility of secular records dedicated
themselves to what was known as the Higher Criticism.
In Germany David Friedrich Strauss laboured until
his death in 1874 to prove that many passages in the
Gospel narratives should be regarded as embodying
'myths' rather than facts. In France Joseph Ernest
Renan compiled an erudite *History of the Origins of
Christianity* in eight volumes (1863–83) to show that the
religious ideas of the Hebrew prophets and the
Church Fathers changed and evolved as the world
about them changed. It was an error, Renan believed,
to ascribe a dogmatic finality to the judgements they

had formulated under the influence of temporal conditions.

The same realistic approach gave a new vigour to historical interpretation. By assuming that the literature, the art, the social customs, and the religious practices of a people were contingent on the level of its culture, the force of inherited traditions, the soil, climate, and food supply, critics set up a naturalistic foundation and a frame by which to measure man's achievements. The French critic and historian Hippolyte Adlophe Taine esteemed this method so highly that it led him to a scientific determinism. He believed that individuals and nations could be anatomized with precision because their thoughts and actions were the inescapable consequence of heredity and environment.

The mood of realism that dominated the second half of the nineteenth century had clearly manifested itself in literature and art by 1870. In fiction the new spirit had already stamped the work of Nikolai Gogol, 'the father of Russian realism', who died in 1852. The same year opened the long literary career of Leo Tolstoy, a career that was to touch its zenith with the publication of *War and Peace* (1866), at the same moment that Feodor Dostoievski completed his *Crime and Punishment*. Literary realism came of age in France with Gustave Flaubert's *Madame Bovary* (1857), although Flaubert did not regard himself as a realist and was dismayed when the work was attacked on the grounds of indecency. The earliest novels of the Goncourt brothers appeared in the 1860's, and Émile Zola, the leading exponent of naturalism, commenced his prolific writing in this decade. In England Charles Dickens's prodigious output continued until his death in 1870. His blend of realism and sentiment, his genius for characterization that often verged on caricature, and his sympathy for the poor and unfortunate had made him the most popular English novelist since Sir Walter Scott. The reaction against early Victorian idealization and sentimentality, already presaged in the satirical novels and parodies of William Makepeace Thackeray, found more sober and conscientious expression in the works of George Eliot (Mary Ann Evans). George Meredith's first success, *The Ordeal of Richard Feverel*, dated from 1859, and Thomas Hardy's series of mordant novels commenced with *Desperate Remedies* in 1871. In drama the outstanding realist of the later nineteenth century was the Norwegian, Henrik Ibsen, whose assaults on bourgeois complacency awakened a succession of reverberations from the presentation of *Pillars of Society* (1877) to *When We Dead Awaken* (1899).

To dumbfound the bourgeois and shock his prudish conventionality was not difficult in an age that made a cult of respectability. The poet and artist were expected to idealize rather than to imitate nature, and those who repudiated academic rules and sought a fresh and more natural approach to their subject-matter invited critical censure. The Pre-Raphaelite Brotherhood (Holman Hunt, Dante Gabriel Rossetti, John Everett Millais) were relatively innocuous as painters, but when their literary colleagues turned to verse, Rossetti, Algernon Charles Swinburne, William Morris, and others were attacked in the *Contemporary Review* as 'The Fleshly

School of Poetry' (1871). The Pre-Raphaelites were realists in their earnest wish to depict life honestly, but realists in very little else; their enthusiasm for medieval art forms and their search for ideal beauty linked them to the Romantic tradition. In France they found a more virile counterpart in the Parnassian School led by Leconte de Lisle and Sully-Prudhomme. The Parnassians strove more consciously and more successfully to adapt their art to the rational and scientific spirit of the age while freeing it from the excessive emotionalism, mysticism, and subjectivism of the Romantic era.

America produced two noteworthy writers of realistic literature in Mark Twain (Samuel Langhorne Clemens) and Walt Whitman. Twain's masterpieces were his picaresque novels, *The Adventures of Tom Sawyer* (1876) and *The Adventures of Huckleberry Finn* (1884), which recaptured, with robust humour and colloquial idiom, the memories of his boyhood in Missouri. Walt Whitman is more difficult to classify; an intense individualist, exuberant, mystical, and romantic in his celebration of democracy, he also produced many passages of gusty blank verse stamped with a stark and authentic realism. At his worst his unrestrained *mélange* of names and images degenerated into banality and his verse read 'like a hardware catalogue'.

The revolt against the pomp and prettiness of academic art influenced European painting from the middle of the nineteenth century onward, and the feud between the academicians and the heretics lasted until its closing decades. Artists who repudiated religious and neo-classical themes to paint ungainly nudes and naturalistic landscapes were rejected by the salons and largely ignored by the public. Gustave Courbet was the first painter who frankly invited the charge of realism. His contempt for precedent and allegory was supreme: 'Show me an angel', he mocked his critics, 'and I will paint one.' His genre pictures captivated young art students in the 1850's and 1860's, and he stood with Edouard Manet in his revolt against the sterile mannerisms of the French salon masters. As painters, however, Courbet and Manet diverged, and the latter became a leader of the impressionist school. Manet's scenes had the sharp focus and arresting fidelity of a photograph, and within its limits his technique remained unsurpassed. But Realism and Impressionism both had limitations, the limitations implicit in the artist himself. If he painted only what he saw, and if what he saw was the reflection of light on the surface of things, that was seldom enough. When the impassioned quarrels that shook the studios and cafés of the Latin quarter for half a century finally died away the painter who came closest to apotheosis was one who had been little regarded: Paul Cézanne.

A friend of Zola, drawn like the novelist to the realistic creed in art, Cézanne patiently analysed and then outgrew the Realists and Impressionists. He laboured to find the geometric in nature, to 'give architecture to the universe', and his experiments in technique laid the foundations for Post-Impressionism and Cubism. His landscapes repelled his contemporaries, but later admirers were to acclaim him as a master who saw beneath the surface and gave an organic structure, a solidity and richness, to natural objects. And what was more important, they came to recognize that his effects were achieved not by slavish imitation but by an intense and arduous *re-creation* of nature.

This rediscovery that the artist was himself the most important element in his art, and that the thinker not only perceived but also imposed form on the objective world, had a significance beyond the sphere of aesthetics. Nineteenth-century thought had been dominated by an increasing faith in the order and continuity of natural processes. The principle of the conservation of matter and the conservation of energy reinforced the tenets of positivism, and materialistic explanations prevailed over theological or metaphysical arguments concerning the nature of the universe and of man. Before the nineteenth century closed, however, investigators on the frontiers of science began to detect some disturbing aberrations that challenged several of the 'immutable' laws upon which the positivists had rested their case. The orderly and self-sufficient universe that had been posited was already dissolving when the century closed, and new thinkers were preparing, like Cézanne, to re-create nature. But the story of this revolution in philosophy and physics belongs to the twentieth century.

Chapter Five

THE FRUITS OF INDUSTRIALISM AND IMPERIALISM (1881-98)

By the close of the nineteenth century mechanized industry had become the most powerful force shaping western civilization. The machines outstripped the intention of their builders, economic materialism overshadowed the age, and Emerson's prophetic warning that 'Things are in the saddle and ride mankind' turned to sober truth. For machine production was dynamic and expansive; its energies outgrew control, transformed the structure of European society, and invaded remoter regions. The primary function of the machines was to pour out a flood of cheap, standardized commodities, but their influence did not end when this primary function was fulfilled: the multiplication of factories brought a rise in the urban proletariat until the armies of socialism threatened the bourgeois state. The quenchless hunger of the iron slaves for more raw materials and wider markets launched the industrial powers on a new campaign of colonial imperialism. The progress of industrialism in the final decades of the nineteenth century bore a direct relation to the growth of the proletariat and the pressure of imperialism and for all three developments power-driven machinery provided the principal moving force.

In peace or war industrial machinery had become

the indispensable instrument, the essential gauge of power. Area and population were no longer the most significant indices of a nation's economic productivity or war potential. Warfare itself was becoming industrialized, and a new ratio of strength had emerged that made manpower insufficient in battle unless it was backed by the tireless energy and prodigious output of a mechanized industry. In this new world of competing imperialisms no nation that lacked a well-developed factory system could long sustain the role of a great power.

This new dispensation by the god of the machine, this revision in the prerequisites of power, had not been fully grasped by political or military observers when the nineteenth century closed. In retrospect it becomes clear that three leading nations had far outrun their rivals in the race to exploit the advantages of an industrial economy. Great Britain had been the 'workshop of the world' for a hundred years, but by 1900 Germany and the United States had cut down the British lead. The resources and industrial equipment of these three countries—Britain, Germany, and the United States—placed them in a special category. They were the super-powers. France, Russia, Austria, and Italy were all great powers but they occupied a secondary position; their industry was not adequate to their needs, although France almost approached the requirements of a super-power. The third category included the remaining states of Europe and the world, from highly industrialized but numerically weak nations like the Belgians with 7,000,000 population, to numerically

strong but industrially negligible empires like the
Chinese with possibly 300,000,000 people. Japan,
though it attracted attention to itself by defeating China
in 1894, was still an unpredictable factor in the later
decades of the nineteenth century. It was shortly to
reveal the awe-inspiring rapidity with which modern
technology could alter the industrial and military status
of an energetic nation.

Not only the possession of industrial machinery but
the manufacture and export of machines became an
index of power by 1880. Britain, the United States, and
Germany were then the principal exporters; together
they produced four-fifths of the machinery sold in the
international market. The three increased their virtual
monopoly up to the First World War, but among themselves there was a significant reversal of rank. In 1880
the order of precedence was Great Britain, Germany,
the United States. By 1913 it had become Germany,
the United States, Great Britain. This relative decline
in the value of British machine exports was an ominous
portent for Great Britain. For the British built almost
half their machinery for sale abroad, whereas the
Germans sent only one-fourth of theirs out of the
country and the Americans only one-tenth. In terms of
total production the discrepancy between the three
leading competitors for world markets had become
highly impressive. By 1913 the United States was
building one-half the industrial machinery of the world,
Germany one-fifth, and Britain one-eighth. The fact
that the Americans kept nine-tenths of their enormous
output of machines at home obscured their extraordin-

ary progress towards industrialization, and the rivalry between Britain and Germany for world trade appeared the most acute. In reality, however, both Germany and Britain had been outstripped in the industrial race by the young giant of the west when the twentieth century opened.

In the 1880's and the 1890's the Anglo-German trade rivalry developed into a duel of titans in which the arithmetic of power recorded a succession of German gains. In 1880–4 German steel mills produced only half as much steel as the British; by 1900 they were producing 20 per cent. more. British exports of cotton manufactures dropped between 1880 and 1900, while German exports doubled. British pig-iron production and consumption remained almost stationary during these twenty years, but German output and consumption increased over 100 per cent. This rivalry in metals and textiles, the strongest branches of British trade, provided a real challenge, but the competition of the German merchant marine stirred the British people even more deeply. Although German shipping tonnage on register remained only one-sixth that of Britain from 1880 to 1900, the lower freight rates on German ships lured manufacturers—and even some British manufacturers—to ship their wares through Hamburg. 'The Germans', *The Times* admitted in 1886, 'are beginning to beat us in many of the qualities which are the factors of commercial success.' Other British obervers, however, remained more optimistic. In 1901 the London *Daily Telegraph* could still declare with confidence: 'What is gone is our monopoly. What is not

gone is our supremacy. There is no decadence.' The
opening of the twentieth century found Britain still
in the lead with 21 per cent. of international trade.
Germany came second with 12 per cent., the United
States third with 11 per cent., and France fourth with
8 per cent. In the next thirteen years world trade doubled
and the percentages shifted, but of the four leading
powers only the United States made a relative gain.
When the First World War commenced the figures
stood: Britain 17 per cent., the United States 15 per
cent., Germany 12 per cent., and France 7 per cent.
Yet it was still the (now stationary) German share of
international trade that most Englishmen viewed with
alarm rather than the more rapid American expansion.

Fortunately for Great Britain the movement of commodities across political frontiers was not the only
important index of economic strength. Nine-tenths of
the international financial transactions were still
carried on in pounds sterling, because the pound remained the most stable unit of exchange. The profits
from banking, insurance, and foreign investments
brought Great Britain an 'invisible' income that helped
to pay for the excess of imports over exports and
preserved British financial leadership. Between 1880
and 1913 British investments abroad multiplied threefold, until a quarter of the national wealth had been
exported. The French foreign investments were only
one-half and the German only one-third the British
total. Furthermore, almost 50 per cent, of British
capital exported went to develop regions within the
empire and could be safeguarded with fair success. The

rate of interest on foreign investments was generally high, but the risk of loss was often high also. When, as sometimes happened, foreign borrowers defaulted on their debts, British, French, or German bondholders might press their government to help them to collect. A considerable share of the capital exported went to politically weak and economically retarded countries and paved the way for the march of imperialism. Small nations in need of financial aid and technological equipment, impoverished peoples whose leaders borrowed heavily from the bankers of London, Paris, or Berlin, might find themselves reduced to a condition of economic vassalage. Their country might even forfeit its political independence and become a protectorate of the great power to which its resources had been pledged.

As business profits mounted and the capital available for investment increased, those with money to lend placed it with investment brokers and might remain almost entirely ignorant of the good or evil that it wrought in domestic or foreign ventures. Investors and bondholders were usually satisfied if their return remained sufficiently high, and they did not inquire too strictly whether the corporation that paid them dividends rewarded its staff equitably or whether the interest they drew from a mine in South America or a trading company in Africa represented a reasonable profit or a pitiless extortion. The widening gulf that separated the rich from the poor, the owners of capital from the workers, increased the evils of 'absentee landlordism' in the capitalistic system. The effect, inevitably, was to depersonalize and dehumanize the relationship between the bondholder and the 'bondservants' whom he might never see.

Within the factory system itself this shift towards finance capitalism weakened the older paternalistic relation between the employer and his workmen. In the early years of the industrial revolution most mills and factories began as private enterprises, and many remained under the direction of a single family for generations. The profits that arose from the business were usually put back to provide for expansion, and a small responsible group of shareholders, closely connected with the business and often personally known to the employees, retained ownership and control. But this type of family industry was outgrown as the nineteenth century advanced. Larger, more impersonal aggregations of stockholders, protected by the statutes governing limited liability companies, tended to supplant the family firm or partnership. In England after the Companies Act of 1844, in France after 1867, in Germany after 1870, corporations with an active board of directors and hundreds or thousands of shareholders multiplied rapidly. Ownership was more widely distributed while management was steadily centralized. Control of a company, or of an entire industry, might come to rest with a handful of men or with a single 'captain of industry' who won a commanding influence. Local shopkeepers felt the encroachment of the chain stores; small foundries and ironworks were swallowed up by the gigantic steel combinations. Free business enterprise, which permitted the development of business corporations, was itself threatened by the tightening monopoly secured by a few aggressive firms. In law the corporation had only the rights of a legal person, but in fact it was potentially immortal and capable of unlimited expansion. An aggressive corporation might absorb or crush its competitors until it dominated a field of economic activity so completely that free business enterprise within that field became a fiction.

A parallel development that sometimes facilitated such concentration of control within an industry was the rise of finance capitalism. In order to expand its activities, or to buy out a competitor, a company might borrow the necessary capital from a firm of bankers, who thus acquired an interest in the company. Occasionally the bankers insisted that a member of their staff be elected chairman of the company in order to watch over the investment. One German bank, for example, had directors on the boards of 200 corporations before 1914. The influence that a great investment trust, with headquarters in London, Berlin, Paris, or New York, might gain in this way could decide events in distant continents, but its activities were a mystery to the man in the street and might extend beyond the ken and the control of local legislators.

By 1900 the growth of large business combinations, known variously as pools, trusts, or cartels, had become a problem to jurists and politicians. Some corporations with monopolistic tendencies became so powerful that it was feared they might evade government control and pursue their quest for profits at the expense of the public welfare and the national interest. Yet it was also recognized that, through the benefits of centralization, they often improved the methods of mass production, stimulated new industries, provided new forms of employment, and promoted prosperity. Men who acquire power are often admired and criticized at the same time. The courage, initiative, and foresight of the business leaders who built vast financial pyramids, developed the resources of a wilderness, and gambled with lives and gold on engineering feats that involved great risks but dazzling rewards, fascinated the new age. Admirers saw these titans as architects of prosperity who asserted humanity's right of eminent domain to exploit the resources of the planet, and, if need be, to enforce the benefits of civilization upon reluctant and unprogressive peoples. But to hostile critics who distrusted the aims and deplored the methods of these international financiers and captains of industry they appeared ruthless and predatory, the 'robber barons' of the modern world. The legal devices and financial legerdemain that obscured the operations of 'big business' were too complex for the common man to grasp, and it was easy for political agitators to play upon his distrust of the 'capitalists' and to magnify their power. Like the god Mercury, patron of commerce, they seemed to abstract the fatness of the fields and the fruits of other men's labour by secret and invisible means.

The nineteenth century closed with all the energies of a dynamic industrial civilization rising to a crescendo. In the economic sphere concentration and centralization appeared to be the dominant principles of the age —concentration of capital, of industry, of population, of power. Throughout Europe and North America the formation of pools, cartels, combines, corporations, trusts, and other devices for merging the directorates of varied business interests, tightened and centralized the control of economic life. The concentration of population was even more noteworthy than the concentration of wealth. In England and Belgium one-half the people were urban dwellers in 1850, three-fourths in 1900. In Germany, where the census had recorded only eight large cities (100,000 inhabitants or more) in 1871, there were thirty-three by 1900 and forty-eight by 1910. Large cities grew faster than small ones, and the towns devoured the villages. By 1900 one out of twenty-five Frenchmen lived in Paris, one out of twenty Germans in Berlin. In England and Wales one-tenth of the inhabitants had been drawn into the vortex of London. Even in the United States, with 3,000,000 square miles to disperse in, nearly one-half the population was concentrated on one per cent. of the land area, and the ten largest cities held one-eighth of the nation.

This expansion of the modern city was closely linked to the growth of the factory system. Modern industry was essentially dynamic, cumulative, and expansive. Under machine production, the unit cost of an article declined as the standardized output rose. It was more profitable, therefore, to aim at a larger and larger body of consumers, to expand production and constantly invade new areas. Steam power assured cheap and regular transportation (the railway mileage of the world quadrupled between 1870 and 1900), and the decline in shipping charges brought into being for the first time in history a world market and a world economy. Raw materials could be brought to the machine from other continents and manufactures exported halfway around the world at rates that allowed them to compete profitably with local wares.

The consequence was sharper competition, and this in turn demanded increased efficiency and production to lower the selling price. Small firms with a limited trade often went under, while large industries branched out, some of them growing to gigantic proportions. In Germany the minor industrial plants (those employing five workmen or less) declined by half between 1880 and 1914, while the larger factories (employing fifty or more workers) doubled in number. A majority of the German industrial labourers were still occupied in small plants at the earlier date, but thirty years later two-thirds were in large factories. The number of industrial units had declined, they were fewer but larger, and they employed four times the total of workers recorded for 1880. Such continued herding of millhands and factory help into fewer but larger combines was common to all the industrialized countries. In general it promoted efficiency, multiplied production, and lowered costs. But it had other effects not intended by the employers and less gratifying to them. In a large company with thousands on its pay-roll the cleavage between the management and the workers tended to widen. The workers became conscious of themselves as a class with separate interests, differing demands, and specific grievances. And they could unite more effectively for collective bargaining as their numbers rose and their working conditions brought them together.

One logical result was the rapid growth of labour unions. By the last quarter of the nineteenth century the laws against workers' organizations had been relaxed. The skilled craftsmen were the first to form craft unions to promote the welfare of their members. Later, many of these unions hastened to federate in large industrial unions, and by 1900 trade union membership reached 2,000,000 in Great Britain and about 1,000,000 in Germany and the United States. The unskilled labourers were more hesitant about organizing, but once their movement began to progress in the 1880's it developed rapidly. Miners, dockers, and factory hands turned to collective bargaining, and large industrial unions appeared in Europe, the United States, and the British self-governing dominions.

With the rise of powerful unions, labour ceased to be a 'commodity' in the world of industry and became in some sense a partner. The workers demanded a more substantial share of the profits and enforced their demand by the threat to strike. Their claims for higher wages had justification, especially after 1895, for prices and living costs, which had been relatively low for twenty years, began a long climb. The rise in real wages between 1880 and 1900 was only 20 to 25 per cent. in Great Britain, Germany, and France, whereas the average worker's productive capacity, thanks to the machines, increased more rapidly, and the proportionate wealth of the capitalist employer rose more rapidly still. The industrial labourer, whose efforts were essential to production, was persuaded that he did not receive a just share of the benefits and profits which the mechanism of industry had made available.

In addition to bargaining directly with their employers, working men could carry their fight into the field of politics; when they did so socialism became an acute political issue. Throughout the later nineteenth century the vote was extended to a larger and larger electorate in all democratic countries, and the disinherited classes grew more powerful when they found that they could oppose the weight of numbers to the influence of privileged minority groups. In the German empire and the French Republic universal manhood suffrage had been granted by 1871; in Switzerland it was embodied in the Federal Constitution of 1874; in Great Britain it was virtually in force after the Reform Acts of 1884–5 which raised the electorate from 3,000,000 to 5,000,000. Spain (1890), Belgium (1893), and Norway (1898) adopted it, and the government of the Netherlands enfranchised all adult males who paid one florin in taxes (1896). An Italian law of 1882 allowed the vote to all males over twenty who had a primary school education and could meet a small property qualification, and universal manhood suffrage followed in 1912. In Austria and Hungary political democracy was delayed by the determination of the German and Magyar minorities to retain their ascendancy, and in most of the Balkan states it was absent or inoperative. Neither the Russian nor the Ottoman empires had a national franchise or even a constitution in 1900, but the Russians were to secure a representative assembly, the Duma, in 1906, and the Young Turks adopted universal manhood suffrage, nominally at least, after their successful revolution shattered the reactionary régime of Abdul Hamid II in 1908.

Had the millions of citizens with low incomes and little or no property been united by their povery they could have carried all elections against the wealthy few. In Prussia, for instance, on the eve of the First World War, the few thousand persons with fortunes that averaged 5,000,000 marks were outnumbered 400 to 1 by the great majority whose worldly wealth averaged less than 25,000 marks *per capita*. For Great Britain comparable statistics suggest that there were 5,000 citizens whose wealth exceeded £100,000, but seven Englishmen out of eight had an average of £100 or less— one-thousandth as much. Political equality did not appear to have brought economic equality nearer, but the unpropertied majority were not of one mind on tariffs, capital levies, and taxes on income, inheritance, or surplus profits. Farmers wanted a fair price for their crops and often welcomed import duties that excluded foreign shipments of grain. City workers, on the other hand, might agitate for the abolition of 'corn laws' in the hope that with free importation the price of bread would fall. Some labour groups felt that their interests set them more sharply against one another than against their employers with whom they shared one common concern: the promotion of the particular industry or enterprise on which all depended for a livelihood.

A conflict of aims divided the urban and rural classes in almost every country. The rural worker tended to remain individualistic, conservative, and orthodox in his religious faith. The urban worker was more readily won to collectivism, more willing to join a union, and more susceptible to materialistic and agnostic doctrines. Cleavages in the ranks of the 'expropriated classes' also developed because of professional pride. Trained mechanics and skilled artisans regarded themselves with reason as the aristocracy of labour and resisted the levelling dogmas that invoked a mechanical equality for all members of society. Every farmer with an acre of land, every worker who owned his home, every foreman promoted to a position of responsibility, had an advantage to safeguard. In addition there was a large middle-class army of white-collar workers, store and office clerks, small shopkeepers, small business men and members of various professional groups, who all enjoyed a social if not an economic status that set them apart from the ranks of organized labour.

These divisions and differences within the working classes help to explain why the socialist parties that were formed in the 1880's and 1890's grew very slowly at first. A period of preparation and education was needed before the masses could become conscious of themselves and of their common ideals and aims. This emergence of the masses, this increasing emphasis on the rights of the common people, slowly shifted the centre of gravity in European society. But it revealed itself first and most positively in the spread of popular education, in the growth of trade unionism, in the formation of co-operative organizations, before it invaded the political arena and compelled the older parliamentary groups to make way for a 'people's party' powerful enough to claim a share in the government.

Until the end of the nineteenth century the lower classes improved their condition chiefly by adopting some of the liberties and benefits that the middle class had already won. There was a steady diffusion through the submerged levels of European society of democratic ideals, liberty of thought and action, economic and educational opportunity, and finally political representation. The growth of craft unionism and then of industrial unionism has already been noted: it enabled the workers to improve their bargaining power and to secure better wages and working hours from their employers. But the spread of popular education and the formation of co-operative societies were equally important as signs of a proletarian awakening. Taking the year 1900 as an approximate dividing line, it may be said that before that date most European workers still sought to improve their condition within the framework of an existing bourgeois democracy. After that date an increasing proportion of the unpropertied classes passed over to the socialist camp. They had come to the decision that the prevailing social and political order was fundamentally iniquitous and that it must be overthrown or radically transformed. This change in attitude was a shift from an evolutionary to a revolutionary philosophy, though many cautious radicals still preferred to shut their eyes to this fact and to think of a socialist revolution as something that could be effected gradually and by constitutional means.

A central tenet of the capitalist creed was the sanctity

of private property. So long as wealth continued to beget wealth and large fortunes remained in the possession of a small minority the accumulation of unearned increments could not fail to perpetuate the economic inequality. Recognition of this fact helped to inspire the co-operative movements that developed strongly in the later nineteenth century. Their founders hoped to subordinate the spirit of competition and profit-making to the general benefit of the members. Consumer co-operatives grew up within the capitalistic system, and the profits of distribution were passed on as dividends to the shareholders. As all who participated were encouraged to purchase a share in the enterprise, all were in some sense employers and employees, capitalists and workers. Producers' co-operatives were in general less numerous and less successful than consumers' co-operatives, but both had the same purpose and inspiration, to dissolve the distinction between capital and labour by fusing the two together. Farmers organized agricultural co-operatives to assemble, grade, pack, preserve, transport, and market their produce. From their contributed capital they founded rural credit banks to minister to their individual needs. In the fields of manufacture and commerce producers' co-operatives turned to processes in which labour was an important element, the making of furniture, clothing, shoes, or soap, and the distributing of them through their own retail stores. In general, prices were fixed at the prevailing levels, and profits were distributed to members in proportion to their share certificates. The co-operative movement spread to all the European countries, and to America, Asia, and Australia. In 1895 an International Co-operative Alliance was formed to advise and encourage new groups. Essentially, the movement was an attempt to develop semi-collectivist cells within the body of a capitalist society, and the members were almost all people of modest circumstances who were seeking a better way to protect themselves from what they regarded as the exploitation of the middleman and the financier.

Fraternal orders or friendly societies of a myriad aims and types also took root, and they multiplied more extensively than the co-operatives. Like the trade unions and the Rochdale Society of Equitable Pioneers (the most permanent form of co-operative store), the 'friendly society' owed much to British initiative. After 1860 the laws governing free associations were simplified throughout western Europe, and lodges, working mens' clubs, and national and international brotherhoods sprang up spontaneously. Their purposes, as defined in their charters, ranged from the convivial to the grim, from social entertainment to care of the maimed, the sick, the blind, and the orphaned, and to burial of the dead. Many societies, and these the most important, offered mutual insurance benefits to their members to help them in facing sickness, accidents, old age, and other dark eventualities that haunt the poor. In Great Britain friendly societies counted 7,000,000 members by 1885 and 14,000,000 by 1910. On the continent of Europe the movement was less pronounced, but various organizations with similar aims, co-operative credit associations, working men's

benefit clubs, and Catholic health, welfare, and insurance circles, made notable gains in funds and
membership during the closing decades of the century.

A mutual benefit association, if it remained active
and solvent, had a steadying influence on its working-
class members. They gained a hardier sense of social
solidarity, and they looked with more favour on the
laws safeguarding private property because their individual premiums and expected benefits were a form
of capital investment. Most men become more conservative when they have something to conserve. In
Britain, where *laissez-faire* ideals were strong, many
workers created insurance funds on their own initiative;
in Germany, with its paternalistic traditions, the state
assumed this responsibility after 1883. Bismarck was
determined to curb the socialists, but he recognized the
validity of their demands for social justice. The industrial and the agricultural labourer, living on a
minimum wage, could seldom make adequate provision
against sickness, disability, and old age. The worker
who ceased to work ceased to earn and might become
destitute within a few weeks or months. It was therefore both prudent and humanitarian for the state to
introduce a system of compulsory insurance that would
provide aid in advance for the unemployed, the aged,
the sick, and the disabled.

Germany was the first great power thus to experiment
with social insurance on a national scale. A Health
Insurance Law, adopted by the Reichstag in 1883,
offered a maximum of thirteen weeks of medical care
in any one year to its beneficiaries. The workers bore

two-thirds and the employers one-third of the cost.
In 1884 an Accident Insurance Law followed, wholly
supported by dues collected from the employers, and
in 1889 the structure was crowned by an Old Age and
Invalidity Law. For the maintenance of this last the
workers, the employers, and the government all contributed, and the magnitude of the state insurance
programme was soon revealed in the official reports.
Between 1885 and 1900 some 50,000,000 benefit claims
were paid under the sickness, accident, and age disability clauses.

Impressed by the German experiment, other nations
introduced similar legislation before the century ended.
Health insurance acts, old age pensions, and compensation for workers injured at their trade, were enforced
in Austria–Hungary. Denmark, Norway, Belgium,
Switzerland, Italy, and France. Even in Great Britain,
where the prejudice against state intrusion into business
and industrial management remained powerful, a
Workmen's Compensation Act was passed in 1897.
The British measure restricted compensation to accidents not caused by the 'gross carelessness of the
worker', a provision that threw many cases into litiga-
tion. In the United States all forms of state insurance
for the working classes lagged, partly because of the
higher economic status of the average worker, but
chiefly because of the individualistic philosophy that
dominated the American way of life. The Australians
and New Zealanders, in striking contrast to most
English-speaking nations, anticipated European labour
legislation; the colony of Victoria set up boards to fix

M

industrial wages in 1885, and the New Zealand Labour party after 1890 embarked on a daring social programme to break up large land holdings, limit private fortunes by a progressive income tax, and protect industrial workers through strict factory laws. The eight-hour day was established by law in 1897 and old age pensions in 1898.

This flood of labour legislation, so swift and so well-nigh universal in the western world, made the 1890's a significant decade in social history. The spirit of the times was obviously changing. Workers' hours, wage rates, health, safety, protection, disability risks and old age pensions were ceasing to be a matter of private concern. The business philosophy of free economic enterprise and unregulated competition, in which the employee and employer met on a basis of voluntary contracts with a minimum of government supervision and regulation, had been tried and found wanting. The state was stepping in, not merely to mediate between capital and labour, but to enforce compulsory arbitration, compulsory insurance, compulsory wage rates, and compulsory pensions to the aged and disabled worker and his dependents. Within a generation this drift towards state socialism was to become an almost irresistible current, driving the peoples of Europe towards a more and more explicit regulation of their social and economic life.

The decline of *laissez-faire* and the growth of economic regimentation could also be measured by the rise of tariff walls that obstructed the free flow of trade and intensified the spirit of economic nationalism. The

1880's brought a powerful swing towards protectionism. To protect themselves from the serious competition of British manufactures and American wheat, European industrialists and farmers urged their governments to fence the national field, and the politicians, always interested in additional revenue, responded promptly by raising import duties. Russia, Spain, and Italy had already increased their tariff legislation by 1878; Germany turned resolutely towards protection in 1879; France and Austria imposed additional rates on imported manufactures in 1881. After 1885 a second wave of protectionist sentiment swept Europe, Germany leading with higher duties on many agricultural products, France matching the measures immediately, Italy following in 1887, and Sweden in 1888. When Switzerland forsook free trade in 1891, only Great Britain, Belgium, and Holland remained loyal in principle to the *laissez-faire* commercial policy that had been so widely endorsed earlier in the century. The United States, where the industrial interests had been in the ascendant since the Civil War, guarded the vast American market with jealous vigilance, erecting a tariff wall in the 1880's that was higher than any in Europe. Even the British dominions broke with *laissez-faire* traditions to follow the general trend, levying import duties on goods from all countries including Britain.

The last quarter of the nineteenth century was a period of unbridled imperialism. All the great powers sought new conquests, and all except Austria–Hungary fought colonial wars to extend their possessions on other continents. One-fifth of the land area of the

globe and one-tenth of its inhabitants were gathered
into the expanding domains of the European conquerors
within a generation, a rate of imperialist encroachment
unsurpassed in history. It was the climax of five centuries of European expansion overseas; by 1900
European civilization overshadowed the earth; and
Joseph Chamberlain summarized this denouement in a
sentence: 'The day of small nations has long passed
away; the day of Empires has come.'

Africa, four times the area of Europe, was parcelled
out in a generation. The race to establish protectorates
throughout its little-known hinterland quickened after
1881 when the French secured Tunis. Disorders in
Egypt afforded an excuse for British occupation of
Alexandria a year later, but Anglo-Egyptian forces
required fifteen years to subjugate the Sudan. The
daring journeys of David Livingstone, Henry M.
Stanley, Savoignan de Brazza, Herman von Wissman,
and other African explorers revealed the riches and
wonders of the Dark Continent. An 'African fever'
seized the imagination of the Europeans as they read
of strange safaris from the Saharan sands to the South
African veldt and from river-haunted lowlands to the
mist-hung Mountains of the Moon. Adventurers made
'treaties' with native kings, diplomats bluffed and
gambled to maintain inflated claims, and colonial
ministers exchanged notes in a mood of rising exasperation.

In 1884, at the initiative of Bismarck and the French
premier Jules Ferry, fourteen nations sent delegates to
Berlin for a conference on African affairs. Rules were

adopted for the suppression of slavery, the free navigation of the Niger and the Congo, and the definition of
'effective occupation'. The powers recognized the Congo
Free State (subsequently a Belgian possession) and
prepared to delimit their rival spheres of influence:
Britain, France, Germany, Italy, Belgium, Portugal,
and Spain came into possession of vast hinterlands
which lay behind the coastal ports they had established,
and the areas they claimed were expanded swiftly until
all Africa had been delimited. Maps of an empty continent changed to a Joseph's coat of coloured patches,
ending the vague romantic cartography described by
Swift, wherein

> . . . geographers, in Afric-maps,
> With savage-pictures fill their gaps;
> And o'er unhabitable downs
> Place elephants for want of towns.

More than once, in the late nineteenth century, competition for African territory brought some of the great
powers close to hostilities. The French annexation of
Tunis in 1881 antagonized the Italians (who coveted
the site of ancient Carthage) and drove them into an
accord with Germany and Austria (Triple Alliance,
1882). An Anglo-French encounter in the Upper Nile
Valley (Fashoda Affair) excited both nations in 1898
to a dangerous degree. Franco-German disputes over
Morocco provoked a series of crises between 1905 and
1912, crises that were resolved by compromises but
increased the international tension.

With the native African peoples the infiltrating Europeans could not avoid a number of local and limited

conflicts. The years from 1880 to 1900 were filled with muted echoes of obscure clashes in desert and jungle, as the Riffs, Senegalese, Hovas, Tuaregs, Ashantis, Basutos, Zulus, Matabeles, and other stubborn tribes fought vainly against the conquering whites. Only the Abyssinians maintained their independence, repulsing in 1887 and 1896 the Italian expeditionary forces that pushed inland from Eritrea. In almost all areas in which the Europeans established control they checked tribal warfare, improved communication and transportation, and sought to curb disease. It is easy to prove that in the protectorates established by the various European governments the officials were not always equal to their great responsibilities and their treatment of the native Africans was sometimes selfish and arbitrary. But to leave Africa and its peoples to unsupervised exploitation by commercial adventurers and the operations of mining and trading companies that would have extorted their own terms from the native rulers and administered their concessions to please themselves might have been incalculably worse.

The pressure of European expansion, regulated or unregulated, was certain to affect all Africa by the close of the nineteenth century. In 1878 little more than one-tenth of the Continent was under the control of European governments; by 1914 they controlled nine-tenths. The largest single bloc was subjugated by the French. Stretching from Algeria to the Ivory Coast and from Senegal to the Anglo-Egyptian Sudan this French African empire had expanded until it constituted an area twenty times the size of France, exceeding in territorial extent even the total of all British African possessions.

The fairest test of the effects of European rule on the Dark Continent would be a comparison of vital statistics before and after the completion of the European hegemony. Unfortunately, nothing that can even loosely be regarded as census statistics are available. By sifting and analysing data from various sources, however, enough evidence has been accumulated to suggest that the native population of Africa before 1880 had been stationary or almost stationary for centuries. More dependable evidence indicates that between 1880 and 1914—the period during which European governments extended their control over most of the continent— the population increased by about one-third. Such a trend suggests that so far as health and life expectancy were concerned European rule brought the Africans very definite benefits.

In South Africa, where the British were to fight the severest colonial war resulting from the 'new imperialism', the chief resistance came not from native tribes but from the descendants of European settlers. Cape Town had been founded by the Dutch in 1652 but the Cape Colony passed under British control during the Napoleonic Wars, and by 1826 its boundaries had been extended to the Orange river. The Boers, as the Dutch colonists were called, resented British interference, and in 1835 some 10,000 of them began a 'Great Trek' northward, setting up a republic beyond the Vaal river. War between the British and Boers in 1842 and 1848 was followed by an attempt at delimitation of territory.

The British recognized the independence of the Transvaal area where the Boers established the South African Republic (Sand River Convention, 1852). The lands north of the Orange river were also left to them and the Orange Free State emerged there after 1854.

The discovery of diamonds (1867) between the Vaal and Orange rivers, and the location of rich gold mines in the Transvaal (1886) altered the economic picture. The British annexed the diamond fields, which had been under the authority of the Orange Free State, in 1871, and six years later they pressed on to annex the South African Republic. The pressure of imperialism had swept aside the Sand River Convention. Boer resentment, already aroused by the British policy of protecting the African natives, became intense, while the British were affronted by the legal and political discrimination to which foreigners (Uitlanders) were subjected in the Boer republics. The proclamation of a German protectorate over an adjacent stretch of the south-west African coast (1884) increased British apprehension, while the agitation of the Uitlanders alarmed the Boers.

In 1890 the vigorous British imperialist Cecil Rhodes, who had made a fortune in the diamond fields, became prime minister of the Cape Colony. He dreamed of a Cape-to-Cairo railway that would traverse Africa from south to north on British territory, but he found a stubborn opponent in the Boer leader, Paul Kruger. Kruger had fought (1880) to make the South African Republic (Transvaal) independent again after Great Britain annexed it in 1877, and in 1883 he became its president. In 1895 Rhodes's friend Dr. Leander Starr Jameson led 600 men into the Transvaal to aid a revolt of the Uitlanders there. Forewarned, the Boers captured the raiders. After four more years of abortive negotiations war broke out in 1899, with the South African Republic and the Orange Free State allied against the British empire.

For two and a half years the Boers maintained the unequal struggle, finally yielding to forces that outnumbered them five to one and accepting British sovereignty in May 1902. They were promised eventual representative government and a grant of £3,000,000 to repair their shattered farms. The outcry against British aggression that arose throughout the civilized world left the British people in a chastened mood, for they had been brought to realize their diplomatic isolation, their unpopularity, and their military unpreparedness. The South African War greatly weakened if it did not altogether destroy the spirit of aggressive self-confidence that had inflamed British pride in the later nineteenth century. Five years after the war ended the Transvaal and the Orange River colony were granted responsible government, and in 1909 the British and Boer provinces were united as a self-governing dominion, the Union of South Africa.

Asia with its far larger population (one-half the human race in 1880) seemed destined to share the fate of Africa in these decades of advancing imperialism. The British already controlled India; their patrols were clashing with Russian outposts in Persia and Afghanistan; Tibet and the Yangtse valley were designated as

potential spheres for their activities; and upper Burma
was annexed as a province of India in 1886. By 1883 the
French completed their conquest of Indo-China from
Cambodia to Tonkin; the Chinese province of Yunnan
was open to their penetration, and the territory of
Kwangchowan became theirs on lease in 1898. In the
north the Russians were building a railway across
Manchuria and waiting only for the collapse of Chinese
authority to press into Mongolia and Sinkiang. China,
the torpid dragon, seemed destined to die the death of
a thousand cuts. It writhed in its sleep but could not
rouse itself to repel the gnawing tactics of its numerous
foes.

Even the Japanese, adopting European formulas of
imperialism along with European technology, joined
the race for Chinese concessions. Attacking their huge
but inert neighbour in 1894 they detached Korea,
annexed Formosa, and almost secured the Liaotung
peninsula. But this last-named prize was also of
interest to the Russians, the Germans, and the French,
and these powers 'persuaded' the Japanese to restore it
to China. The successes won by the Japanese in the
Sino-Japanese war of 1894 precipitated a further rush
for concessions. All the powers demanded, and all
except Italy received, additional leases, treaty ports,
commercial privileges and indemnities, until their greed
finally aroused the Chinese to resistance. In 1900 a
secret society, the 'Literary and Patriotic Order of
Harmonious Fists' (anglicized as Boxers), murdered
missionaries and traders and besieged the European
legations. This ill-planned attempt to expel the 'foreign

devils' from China brought swift and indiscriminate reprisals. An international army marched on Peking, sacked the palace of the reactionary Empress Tzu Hsi who had encouraged the Boxers, and levied a heavy indemnity. Among the twelve powers that collaborated in this resettlement of Chinese affairs were Japan and the United States.

Unlike most of the other participants that took a share in crushing the Boxer Rebellion, the United States held no territory and claimed no sphere of influence on the mainland of Asia. But the Americans had come into possession of the Philippine islands in 1898 after a brief war with Spain, and had annexed the Hawaiian islands the same year. Although the immediate cause of the Spanish-American War had been a revolt of the Cubans (who were speedily liberated from Spanish domination) the conflict marked a turning-point in American and world affairs. For it signalized the emergence of the United States as a world power, despite the fact that the American people were slow to realize that their long-cherished isolation was at an end. Still absorbed in the gigantic task of exploring and exploiting their own continent, they had attempted to shun adventures beyond the seas. With the acquisition of the Philippines and Hawaii, however, they (or at least their government) recognized the need for a two-ocean navy and an inter-oceanic canal at Panama to permit the speedier reinforcement of either fleet. The Pacific had become an ocean of destiny: the opening of the twentieth century found the battleships of six great powers—Britain, France, Germany, Russia, Japan, and

the United States—cruising in Far Eastern waters. Of
these watchful guardians of oriental affairs, the two
powers most vitally interested in the status of China
were Japan and Russia, for both had territory bordering
on the Sea of Japan. Their rivalry for a dominant influence in north China was to bring the two into armed
conflict by 1904.

The progress of western technology, which had
changed man's way of life more radically in the nineteenth century than in the preceding two thousand
years, continued to accelerate as the century ended.
Newer metals, copper, tin, zinc, aluminium, were in
rising demand for a machine-dominated economy, but
iron still ruled the industrial world. Between 1880 and
1900 the steel production of the globe soared from
4,000,000 to 28,000,000 metric tons, the output of pig
iron from 18,000,000 to 39,000,000. With iron available
in quantity, engineers applied it to novel structural
purposes, notably bridge building and architecture.
The Forth Bridge, the Brooklyn Bridge, the Eiffel
Tower, and the first skyscrapers in Chicago and New
York were completed in the 1880's. The compound
steam turbine, perfected by Sir Charles Parsons in 1891,
revolutionized steam engineering and raised the power
available for electric generators and ocean transport.
Electricity opened new paths in industry and metallurgy, providing power for lathes and elevators, reducing metals in the electric furnace, welding them with
the electric arc, refining and plating them by electroly-
sis. The inorganic chemists created new commercial
products in their laboratories almost overnight, the

most spectacular being the German development of synthetic dyes from coal-tar residues. British manufacturers began the production of cheap wood-pulp paper; a French scientist exhibited the first artificial silk made from cellulose at the Paris Exposition of 1889; and German chemists learned to fix the nitrogen of the air and to synthesize the nitrates indispensable for fertilizers—and for explosives.

In pure as distinguished from applied science (the distinction was rapidly dissolving in actuality) the most fateful advances of this period were made in the study of radioactivity. Although the full significance of the advance was not realized immediately, Wilhelm Konrad Röntgen (German) opened a new era in physics with his detection of X-rays in 1895. The following year Antoine Henri Becquerel (French) discovered that uranium gave off rays similar to those observed by Röntgen, and in 1898 Pierre Curie (French) and Marie Curie (Polish) isolated radium. This international quest into the secrets of matter had been precipitated by Heinrich Hertz (German), whose investigation of the electromagnetic theory of light first propounded by Clerk Maxwell (British) enabled him to demonstrate the existence and measure the velocity of electromagnetic waves as early as 1886.

That such abstract calculations and experiments, seemingly as remote as the stars from the world of practical affairs, had in fact a direct commercial utility was swiftly demonstrated by Guglielmo Marconi. This Irish-Italian inventor utilized 'Hertzian Waves' (as radio waves were still called) to transmit messages, and wireless telegraphy was born (1895). Within three years messages had been successfully transmitted across the English Channel and within six across the Atlantic Ocean. It was a foretaste of the marvels that might be expected from the new science of telecommunication.

The impact of the new technology was changing the face of nature and the fate of man, but the esoteric formulas of the scientists remained arcana to the multitude. Natural science had made incalculable strides in the century and a half since Benjamin Franklin drew electricity from the heavens by flying a kite in a thunderstorm. The promethean fire of heaven had been harnessed to drive man's engines, to hurl his words across the ocean, and to probe the secrets at the heart of matter. To express the laws, compute the relations, and classify the phenomena detected by physicists and chemists, the mathematicians had elaborated their discipline throughout the nineteenth century, adding novel refinements to the laws of motion divined by Sir Isaac Newton and exploring the possibilities of non-Euclidean geometry. Modern mathematics, the most original creation of the human mind, had become an international language, the language, as Galileo had boldly insisted four centuries earlier, in which Nature wrote her secrets. Yet it remained, like the hieratic symbols of the ancient priesthoods, a script that only a small company of initiates could decipher. The scientists formed a select and emancipated fellowship. Segregated by their intent specialization, dedicated to their recondite mysteries, they had outdistanced the lagging march of western civilization.

Nineteenth-century society was fascinated by the triumphs of its scientists and technicians, but it was a fascination of the mind only; the heart remained loyal to an older and humanist tradition. 'We admire with awe', Matthew Arnold admitted to the heralds of a new scientific order,

> We admire with awe
> The exulting thunder of your race;
> You give the universe your law,
> You triumph over time and space!
> Your pride of life, your tireless powers,
> We laud them, but they are not ours.

European thought was still dominated by literary patterns that had been reaffirmed with the Renaissance and perpetuated for five centuries by the rule of the graphocracy. As Inspector of Schools, Arnold fought for the ancient literatures against the intrusion of the new sciences into the curriculum. Emphasis on the literary classics as the core of conventional instruction had made education almost synonymous with book learning, hardening the European mind to the cast of a typographical culture. When, in the later nineteenth century, the still unlettered majority were invited to share the cake of culture, they were prescribed the type of liberal education admired by a leisured class. Instruction proceeded almost entirely on the intellectual plane with scant regard for the practical problems the pupils must face in later life in the field or factory, office or shop, nursery or kitchen, where most of them were destined to labour.

With literacy as the accepted yardstick, the progress

of popular education in the nineteenth century was
measured by the decline in the percentage of illiterates.
Statistics are incomplete and standards variable, but it
seems reasonably clear that a majority of the European
people were still unable to read and write when the
century closed. Figures available for England show
one-third of the men and one-half the women illiterate
in 1840; in France and Belgium one-half the adult
citizens were in the same condition in 1850; in Germany
and the Scandinavian states standards were higher; but
in Italy, Spain, Portugal, Austria, Russia, and the
Balkan countries only one person in ten could be
accounted literate in 1860.

The progress of political democracy made popular
education a critical issue, for it appeared dangerous to
give the franchise to citizens unable to read and write.
James Madison, fourth president of the United States,
emphasized this predicament with the trenchant warning that 'popular government without popular education
is the prologue to a farce or a tragedy'. Almost all
European governments made some provision for free
public schools at the primary level during the last third
of the nineteenth century, Austria–Hungary (1868–9),
Great Britain (1870), Germany (1872), Switzerland
(1874), Italy (1877), the Netherlands (1878), Belgium
(1879), and France (1878–82). Illiteracy declined with
remarkable rapidity. By 1900 it had fallen below 5 per
cent. in Germany, Scandinavia, Britain, and France,
thus ceasing to be a serious problem in north-western
Europe. Southern and eastern Europe still presented a
darker picture. One-third of the population of Austria–

Hungary, one-half of the Italians, two-thirds of the Spaniards and Portuguese, and four-fifths of the Balkan and Russian peoples were unable to read and write when the nineteenth century ended. This meant, taking Europe as a whole, that one-half of the population remained illiterate. In the United States the rate of illiteracy for those over ten years of age fell from 17 per cent. to 10 per cent. between 1880 and 1900, but in Latin America it remained in general exceptionally high, exceeding 90 per cent. in Mexico, Brazil, and Bolivia.

The unprecedented increase in the total reading public throughout western Europe and North America created an ever-widening field for popular journalism to exploit. The number of newspapers in Europe doubled between 1880 and 1900. New inventions— the linotype, monotype, straight-line press, automatic feeder and binder, half-tone photo engraving, and colour presses—reduced costs and multiplied circulation, aided by the substitution of wood-pulp for rag paper. News gathering was speeded by the more rapid transmission of mail and the extension of telegraph and telephone lines. With millions of readers gleaning their knowledge of current events from the penny newspapers, the techniques of propaganda and advertising evolved rapidly and public opinion was given capricious turns. Politicians learned to heed and sometimes to manipulate the oracle of the press; and the right to speak and write freely on public questions became a cardinal principle of the democratic faith.

Under this growing stimulus printing and publishing

N

activities expanded phenomenally. In Germany, long a leader in the book trade, the printing plants doubled their output in twenty years. Wherever literacy increased, new public libraries, reading rooms, book shops, and book stalls strewed volumes, periodicals and pamphlets before the public, catering to its shifting caprices. The heritage of European civilization, in so far as it could be contained in books, was brought within reach of the literate classes, a liberation and an invitation to learning that speeded the democratization of western culture. The common man became aware of a world beyond his former limited horizon, and he acquired a knowledge of social and national questions that prepared him more adequately for the role of an active citizen. Literacy thus provided an indispensable foundation for the spread of democracy in the western world. For as Nicolai Lenin learned in his earliest attempts to arouse the Russian masses, without literacy 'there can be no politics, there can be only rumours, gossip, and prejudice'.

The literature of the late nineteenth century was a mirror in which coming developments cast their shadow before. At the bottom of their inkwells writers saw in cloudy vision the coming disintegration of the bourgeois synthesis, beheld the genii of science, obedient yet terrifying, rise like an incalculable cloud, and deepest of all caught the pale reflection of their own disenchanted faces, each man seeking the riddle of his inner real self. These three recurrent themes—social justice, science, and the inner self—provide a clue to the mood of European literature at the close of the nineteenth century.

A conviction that society had outgrown the drawing-room politics of the Victorian Compromise, and that the genteel tradition in art left too much unsaid about life, had inspired the realist revolt of the 1860's and 1870's. But writers like Émile Zola and Henrik Ibsen, however just their insight and pitiless their pens, were not made to lead a popular revolution. A vital proletarian literature did not develop until socialism had become a more powerful political force. Yet a warning that all was not for the best in the best possible of bourgeois worlds had been sounded by Henry George in *Progress and Poverty* (1879); it was repeated more movingly by Gerhard Hauptmann in *The Weavers* (1892), and echoed from the underworld dives depicted in the early stories of Maxim Gorki. In Britain the formation of the Fabian Society in 1883, which enlisted the support of Sidney Webb and George Bernard Shaw, was a prophetic step, for its members aimed at 'the reorganization of society by the emancipation of land and industrial capital from individual and class ownership . . .'. From his earliest novels and plays, published in the 1880's and 1890's, Shaw revealed his ability to make socialism dangerous by making it amusing. He set himself to puncture by his incisive ridicule the inflated pretensions of British superiority, bourgeois superiority, and masculine superiority, and few of those who laughed at his thrusts realized that the deflation of these confident premises would loose the fountains of the social deep.

Modern technology, that was casting its shadow across so many fields of man's endeavour in the late nineteenth century, affected the manufacture of books more rapidly than it influenced the minds of their authors. The high literary tradition continued to feed itself upon the past, and the masters of *belles lettres* ignored as long as possible the vulgar intrusion of the machines. Even in popular journals the space devoted to scientific inventions and discoveries remained inadequate to their importance when the century closed, partly because the methods and personalities of the scientists were difficult to simplify or to dramatize. But adventure stories with a pseudo-scientific background grew in favour (Jules Verne had raised this type of writing to respectability in the 1860's), and romances laid in the brave new world to be created by science vied with the historical novel in popular appeal. By a strange liaison the new science fiction became involved with utopianism, and a hybrid literature emerged that combined social fantasy with scientific features. Samuel Butler's *Erewhon* (1872) depicted an ideal commonwealth in a manner that made the book a satire on contemporary England. Edward Bellamy's *Looking Backward* (1887), written in a more popular and kindly vein, sold a million copies. William Morris's *News from Nowhere* (1891), Herbert George Wells's *War of the Worlds* (1898), and similar products of sociological idealism enjoyed wide popularity. On the continent one of the most influential novels of this genre was *Freiland, ein soziales Zukunftsbild* (1890), an imaginary account of the foundation of a socialistic colony in equatorial Africa, written by the Austrian journalist and economist Theodor Hertzka.

That bourgeois society was sick some of its own more discerning sons had detected for themselves before 1900. From Scandinavia to Spain writers turned their attention increasingly to social criticism as the nineteenth century neared its close, but there is space to mention only a few representative names. In Norway Björnstjerne Björnson, in Denmark Georg Brandes, in Holland Edward Douwes Dekker and his disciples who founded *De Nieuwe Gids* in the 1880's, in France Émile Zola and Anatole France, in Germany Nietzsche, Hauptmann, and the feminist Louise Otto-Peters, in Italy Edmondo De Amicis, in Spain Ricardo Macías Picavea and Ángel Ganivet—all were disturbed by the symptoms of decadence that they discerned around them but few supplemented their diagnosis by a constructive programme for social recuperation.

Meanwhile there were growing indications of a coming revolt against positivism, intellectualism, and scientific determinism. Science was turning sensitive artistic natures back upon themselves, verifying Coleridge's dictum uttered early in the century that 'Poetry is not the proper antithesis to prose but to science'. Poetry and science could not, in truth, be easily reconciled. It is one of the singular lacunas of modern literature that the epic achievements of the scientists have never been celebrated fittingly in epic verse. The wonder-workers who created enough legends to stock a modern mythology, who bent the lightning to their will, weighed the sun with a slide rule, and exorcized invisible armies of death with the wave of a test-tube, found no bards to praise them in immortal song.

This dichotomy in western culture between the makers of things and the makers of songs ran deeper than a chance intellectual estrangement. The generation that came of age in the 1890's was ripe for disillusionment. It had grown to maturity in an era of great material achievement but in an atmosphere chilled by what Disraeli had well termed 'the frigid theories of a generalizing age'. It was the first generation to realize sharply that science had plunged humanity down an unknown road. A shock went through the confident ranks as the vanguard slowed, seeking the milestones that were not there. The literature of the period records this faltering of morale, the change from inherited optimism to introspective doubt that came with *la fin du siècle*, as if a chill wind had struck from the untravelled wastes of the new century.

Modern man was outgrowing the intoxication of his triumphs and feeling the weight of his desolate and incommunicable singularity. Like the enigmatic hero of Joseph Conrad's early novel, *Lord Jim* (1900), he still obeyed an inherited pattern of conduct. But he was an exile from his own past, an unwitting victim of dark powers, an eternal wanderer, 'excessively romantic' and 'inscrutable at heart'. Like Lord Jim he seemed destined to pass away under a cloud, leaving no one certain what it was he sought.

'Within!' This challenge, raised by Miguel de Unamuno to rally his fellow Spaniards after the defeats of 1898, had a wider, an international significance. 'Those who cannot remember the past are condemned to epeat it', George Santayana warned almost at the same moment. The admonitions were well timed. To take bearings for the road ahead the Europeans had to re-survey the road behind and to reappraise themselves and their traditions. The intellectual confusion of the age resulted in great part from the schism between theology and science, and a number of ardent minds set themselves to seek a reconciliation that would make man 'whole' again. After 1885 the idealist schools of philosophy attracted new converts. Several leading scientists, notably the French mathematician Henri Poincaré, suggested that scientific laws might prove to be relative and statistical, and that mental processes were not reducible to the same terms as physical phenomena. This belief found its ablest defender in Henri Bergson, who insisted in his *Essai sur les données immédiates de la conscience* (1889) that subservience to the external world deadened the mind by reducing its activities to a standardized, mechanistic pattern.

The concept of relativism weakened the position of the positivists and determinists. Walter Pater, who died in 1894, had already observed this trend. 'To regard all things and principles of things as inconstant modes or fashions', he admitted, 'has more and more become the tendency of modern thought.' Those who craved certitude were moved to seek it in other disciplines than science; some turned to 'art for art's sake', and some to religion. Leo XIII, who had succeeded the obdurate Pius IX in 1878, welcomed the opportunity presented by the shift in opinion. Without compromising Catholic tradition, he suggested the possibility of reducing the discrepancies between the religious and the rationalist interpretations of history, and he threw open the Vatican archives to accredited scholars in the faith that with deeper understanding contradictions might be found to harmonize. Ecclesiastics stressed the social welfare of the masses as a field in which Church and state had a joint interest. Sceptics were reminded that the opposition between science and religion was not absolute, and that the careers of Gregor Mendel and Louis Pasteur showed that it was possible to be a great scientist and a good Catholic at the same time. The close of the nineteenth century not only brought a Catholic revival in literature; it found the Church functioning with renewed vigour on many fronts, to the surprise of agnostics who had been prepared, a generation earlier, to predict its imminent collapse.

Those who were indifferent to religion sought other clues to the riddle of the inner self. In the naturalistic atmosphere that western man had come to breathe during this materialistic age the neurotic turned to psychology for relief, and the artist became, almost inevitably, something of a psychologist. He found no lack of pathological subjects. The uprooting of millions caused by the migration to the cities, the falling birthrate that weakened family life and changed the only child from an anomaly almost to a norm, the precarious economic status of the wage-earner, all combined to destroy the emotional security of the average citizen. Lonely in a crowd he concentrated his thoughts upon himself.

This narcissistic drive, this subjectivism, soon reflected itself in art. Expressionism, the practice of giving free expression to one's inner thoughts and sensations, became an accepted technique; the term was first applied to a style of painting but spread to literature and drama. The interior monologue, the stream of consciousness' novel, the search for new symbols and for a unique personal vocabulary, revealed the growing absorption of the newer writers with inner states of thought and feeling. The pyschological novel was not new but it was brought to a new stage of refinement. Henry James, who commenced his long series of novels, dramas, and essays in the 1870's, dissected his characters with unrivalled subtlety and psychological insight. In the 1880's Maurice Barrès commenced a trilogy to which he gave the significant title *Le Culte du moi*, increasing the vogue of psychological individualism, and in *Les Déracinés* (1897) he coined a term that fittingly described the many uprooted drifters of his generation.

Philosophy as well as psychology lent itself to the revolt against a strictly intellectual and rational explanation of experience. The tenets of Pragmatism, as elaborated by Charles S. Peirce (who introduced the word about 1875) and by William James, suggested that the true is 'only the expedient in our way of thinking' and that will and interest rather than the exigencies of logic determine man's rationalizations and beliefs. In simplified form the Pragmatic principle that an idea is true if it works could be readily assimilated with Darwinism, 'true' ideas being those which helped the individual or the group to survive in the unceasing struggle for existence. Business leaders had already cited the doctrine of the 'survival of the fittest' as a justification for unregulated competition, and found its implication that the fittest survive a pleasing reflection on their own supremacy. But there were other more dangerous implications in Darwinism and Pragmatism, for these philosophies might be invoked to support the conclusion that will-power (voluntarism) and driving power (energism) counted more effectively in the effort to survive than the dictates of reason or the refinements of logic. Such arguments offered comfort to the depressed classes because they implied that victory in the social struggle might be decided, not by logic or legal casuistry, but by mass determination and naked force. Nietzsche had stressed the amoral nature of power, insisting that the born leader, the superman, must act with the impersonal ruthlessness of a natural force because he was 'beyond good and evil'. The leaders of a militant proletariat, aspiring to social control, digested the conclusion. To wield power it was necessary to be ruthless.

Ideas are weapons, and the circulation of ideas like those of Marx and Nietzsche were storm warnings. An era of profound social upheavals was approaching. The nineteenth century had seen European society sweep forward like a mighty river broadening and deepening with each decade, turbulent at times but reasonably obedient to its dikes and never catastrophically destructive. The vigorous and intelligent rule of a benevolent bourgeoisie had favoured a remarkable degree of social order, and the *pax Britannica* had helped to preserve a balance of power among the nations.

Wealth, population, standards of living, popular education, and public health had made advances never equalled hitherto by any empire on any continent. Though the force of organized religion had declined, the spirit of humanitarianism had expanded; no age had done more for the common man, or shown more respect for the sanctity of treaties and of contracts. But the nineteenth century, with its order and security, was near its close. Such golden centuries have been rare in the annals of mankind, and no two have ever followed in immediate succession.

Chapter Six

RISING SOCIAL PRESSURES AND
THE BALANCE OF POWER (1898–1914)

WHEN the twentieth century opened in 1901 the European powers had been at peace for thirty years, and there had been no general European war in eighty-five years. All the leading nations except Russia had created the machinery for parliamentary government, although in Germany and Austria–Hungary this machinery did not always function and ministries might defy a majority of the popular representatives and remain in office despite votes of no confidence from the lower chamber. Grave problems existed, social and internal tensions were increasing, but faith in progress and reason was strong, and most people believed their political machinery adequate to resolve the strains by timely readjustments. In this they were mistaken. The problems were not solved. In 1914 the disruptive forces within European society escaped control and the continent was plunged into a disastrous struggle that reduced its population and left its economy shattered. The outbreak of this First World War marked the close of an historical epoch. When the relative equilibrium that had endured since 1815 broke down in 1914, the 460,000,000 inhabitants of Europe entered a new era of violent conflicts, economic collapse and social revolution. Those who survived learned to look back with regret to the years before

1914 as a happier age of decency and order and security.

It is difficult for readers of a later generation to retrace the history of the European nations from 1898 to 1914 without feeling at each step the approach of a tragic denouement, a climax unintended and unforeseen by the actors of the drama. In retrospect, this sense of dramatic irony tends to invest all the decisions taken in those closing years with a quality of doom and to make the outcome appear inescapable. Such a reading is of course a falsification, a dramatization, of the past. But it is not a falsification to affirm that after 1900 signs multiplied in Europe that a grave climax could not be long postponed. The driving forces of European economy had begun to slip their yokes; their masters, reduced to servants, understood these growing forces too imperfectly to curb their acceleration; the political and diplomatic controls were no longer adequate to the increasing strains. Technology, industry, political and economic nationalism were all generating powerful but uneven and sometimes contrary thrusts. In a word, European civilization was threatened by a growing disparity between 'strong physics and weak sociology'.

In such a society there were two principal areas where friction could accumulate sufficiently to set off an explosion. Deepening class antagonism within each troubled nation might lead to a revolution. National rivalry between the more and more heavily armed states might precipitate a war. As it happened, no important European government was overthrown by an internal upheaval in the decades before 1914, largely because the statesmen in every country made adroit concessions to the discontented masses. This search for social justice was the most significant drive in the domestic politics of the European peoples from 1898 to 1914. In the pragmatic sense the quest for social justice was successful: revolutions were avoided. How they were avoided can be explained only by analysing each state separately, because no two had identical patterns or programmes.

In Great Britain the political pattern from 1895 to 1914 broke into two parts, a decade of Conservative rule (1895–1905) followed by a period of Liberal ascendancy (1906–14). The Conservatives came to power in 1895 with the aristocratic Robert Cecil, Marquess of Salisbury, as prime minister and the forceful Joseph Chamberlain as colonial secretary. Chamberlain headed a splinter group of 'Liberal Unionists' who had deserted Gladstone and the Liberal party to join the Conservatives because they were determined to preserve the union with Ireland. A mood of nationalism and imperialism was stirring the British people. The Diamond Jubilee of Queen Victoria in 1897 was celebrated with great pomp, reminding them of the unparalleled progress and prosperity Great Britain had known through the queen's long reign. Chamberlain tried to direct this pride and elation into a positive programme, demanding closer imperial ties with all parts of the empire, larger armaments, and an intrepid foreign policy. In Africa the ardent apostle of Anglo-Saxon supremacy, Cecil Rhodes, predicted an all-British railway from Cairo to Cape Town, a project that fired the imagination of the expansionists. 'I would annex the planets if I could', Rhodes declared with characteristic ardour.

The South African War (1899–1902), for which Britain proved unprepared, dissipated some of this enthusiasm for imperialism, for although the Boer farmers were finally defeated the war was costly to Britain in money and prestige. To raise more revenue and cement the empire more solidly Chamberlain proposed a protective tariff with imperial preference. But import duties on food and manufactures, which might have built an economic fence around the empire and helped British manufacturers to compete against the 'protected' industries of Germany and the United States would also have raised the cost of living for British workers. Tariff Reform was hotly discussed and the issue split the Conservative party, now under the lead of Arthur James Balfour. In 1905 the Liberal leader, Sir Henry Campbell-Bannerman, took office at the head of a new ministry, and an election in 1906 confirmed the Liberal ascendancy. The British electorate had repudiated Tariff Reform and turned away from the nationalist-imperialist-protectionist programme Chamberlain had propounded.

The Liberal government, in alliance with the Labour party, attacked the social question energetically. In 1906 a Workmen's Compensation Act laid the responsibility for the workers' welfare squarely upon the employers, establishing compensation benefits for those workers who were injured or incapacitated at their labour. An Old Age Pensions Act (1908) set up annuities for workers reaching the age of seventy, the funds to be drawn from the national exchequer. In 1909 a Minimum Wage Law established boards to fix the basic remuneration for certain poorly paid occupations, and this measure was extended to include the vital coal industry with its million workers three years later.

'The root trouble of our social system', declared David Lloyd George, who became chancellor of the exchequer in 1908, 'is the precariousness of living.' In 1911 he introduced a National Insurance Act to provide compulsory insurance for workers against sickness, invalidity, and unemployment. The beneficiaries were required to contribute premiums towards some of these funds, but a heavy share of the load fell upon the employers and the national treasury.

To balance the expanded budget Lloyd George proposed extra levies, in particular a graduated income tax, an increased inheritance tax, and a special assessment on the 'unearned increment' resulting from rising land values when such rises profited the owner unduly. This Lloyd George budget of 1909 passed the Commons, but was defeated in the Lords. Thereupon the Liberal government that had sponsored it appealed to the electorate and was returned to office with a reduced majority. The budget became law, and after a second appeal to the voters the House of Lords was shorn of its power to block financial measures, though it could still hold up other bills for as long as two years (Parliament Act of 1911). The will of the popular majority had triumphed against the conservative groups, but class antagonism had been sharpened in the struggle.

More serious still, a crushing burden had been imposed on the treasury and the taxpayers. Coming at a time when international tensions were increasing, this diversion of revenue to social services created difficulties, because it reduced the sums available for imperial defence. This other side of the picture—the problem of national security as contrasted with the problem of social security—will be examined later.

The adoption of these 'Liberal Reforms' in Great Britain after 1905 was in some sense a 'peaceful revolution'. The Liberals were the traditional reform party, but they were driven leftward after 1906 by labour pressure. The British working classes had been disposed to neglect politics until 1901, but in that year a judicial ruling of the House of Lords (Taff Vale Judgement) imperilled the trade unions and rallied workers to the newly-founded Labour party. In the elections of 1906 this party won twenty-nine seats in the House of Commons and increased them to forty-two in 1910. The Liberal cabinet wished to hold the support of these Labour members, and it adopted Labour (that is Socialist) proposals. Hitherto Great Britain had lagged behind most advanced continental countries in social legislation, but after 1906 it caught up and even surpassed them in such innovations as unemployment insurance.

In the Third French Republic a turning-point in the long struggle between Right and Left was reached in the Dreyfus Affair. Captain Alfred Dreyfus, a French Jew, was pronounced guilty of treason by a military court in 1894 and sentenced to life imprisonment in the penal colony on Devil's Island. Four years later the

o

accumulation of evidence pointing to his innocence forced a reopening of his case despite the haughty opposition of the French high command. The French people were profoundly stirred, dividing into Dreyfusards and Anti-Dreyfusards.

The final dramatic revelation that Dreyfus was the victim not merely of a judicial error but of a sustained conspiracy discredited a number of army leaders, anti-Semitic journalists, and other prejudiced groups that had insisted upon his guilt. The parties of the Right were repudiated at the polls, and a 'republican bloc' based on the Centre and Left won control of the Chamber of Deputies and dominated French politics after 1899.

The army staff had long been a stronghold of royalist, reactionary, and Catholic sentiment: it was now republicanized. The authority and influence of the Catholic Church in France was weakened by an Associations Law (1901) that dissolved the religious orders engaged in teaching: public education was laicized. The concordat of 1801, that had governed the relations of Church and State in France for a century, was abrogated (Separation Law, 1905), and the state assumed the ownership of all Church property. In practice, the law was eased, and religious congregations continued to use the churches for worship by arrangement with the local authorities. The principal consequences of the reform crusade were the divorce of religion and politics, the triumph of the republic over its Catholic and royalist opponents, and the virtual elimination of royalism as a vital force in French political life.

The weakening of royalism, militarism, and Catholicism brought a relative strengthening of socialism. The Republican Bloc needed support from the Left for its attack on the citadels of the Right, and it brought this support by a series of social reforms. A Factory Law reduced the working day to eleven hours (1900), then to ten hours (1906), and finally to eight hours for minors (1907). Some measure of compensation for workers injured or disabled at their trade was authorized in 1898, and successive pension laws provided aid for the indigent aged until almost all occupations had been covered by 1910.

To most French workers these limited concessions did not appear sufficient. Socialist agitation mounted steadily. Ideological disputes divided the various socialist groups, but they managed to elect a total of 50 members to the Chamber of Deputies in 1890, 54 in 1906, 76 in 1910, and 101 in 1914. A United Socialist party was organized in 1905.

French workers were more interested in politics than the British and more revolutionary in temper than the Germans. Their labour unions (*syndicats*) used the strike as a political as well as an economic weapon, and their leaders spoke of the day when the solidarity of the working classes would be such that a nation-wide strike would force the bourgeois government to abdicate. To link the various *syndicats* under a unified command a *Confédération Générale du Travail* was created in 1895, and in 1906 its leaders called a general strike for an eight-hour day. The government of the French Republic found itself facing an organization (the C.G.T.) so powerful that it threatened to become a state within the state. But the people of France as a whole, while sympathetic towards labour, were not ready for a working-class revolution: 'the heart of the French bourgeois is on the left,' as André Siegfried was to note wittily, 'but his pocket book is on the right.' The cabinet, headed by the energetic Georges Clemenceau, ordered the police to arrest leading syndicalist officials, and the strike was abandoned. Four years later a graver crisis faced the government when the railway workers walked out, but the cabinet mobilized army reservists to run the trains, and once more the threat of a paralysing strike that would make the labour committee a virtual dictatorship was frustrated. Thereafter, syndicalism as a revolutionary force tended to decline, although membership in the C.G.T., which rose from 200,000 in 1906 to 400,000 in 1912, reached 500,000 in 1914.

In Germany the rapid evolution of the Social Democratic party was more impressive than the slow growth of the Labour party in Britain or the doctrinaire debates of the United Socialists in France. Bismarck's repressive laws against the socialists were allowed to lapse after 1890, when the new emperor, William II, relieved the Iron Chancellor of his office. William was talented, ambitious, impulsive, and inept. His ideal of government was a sort of paternal despotism founded on popularity; he wanted to be admired by his subjects; and he believed that he could charm the German masses into obedience without coercion. But his successive chancellors—the conscientious Caprivi, the septuagenarian Prince von Hohenlohe, the pliant Prince von Bülow, the earnest but ill-starred Bethmann-Hollweg—were not men of Bismarck's stamp. German imperial policy in the Wilhelmian era lacked the unity of direction Bismarck had maintained, becoming more erratic and confusing as rival policy-making cliques jockeyed for power. The ambiguity in the German constitution that left the imperial chancellor and his ministry responsible to the emperor but condemned them to work out legislation with a frequently hostile Reichstag remained unresolved. And policies none too well co-ordinated at best were in constant danger at critical moments from William's headstrong interference and love of histrionic gestures.

In the Reichstag the forces of opposition were headed by the Social Democrats. As the acceleration of German industry multiplied the legions of urban workers, the strength of the Social Democratic party mounted surprisingly. By 1912 it had 110 deputies in the Reichstag, the largest single political bloc, representing some 4,250,000 electors. Twice in 1913 the Social Democrats joined with other dissidents to muster a majority vote, declaring that the Reichstag lacked confidence in the government. But the chancellor did not resign. Nor did the opposition force the issue: few German socialists were revolutionaries. They had extorted a number of concessions for the workers from 1890 onwards—limitation of working hours, improvement in factory conditions, expansion of the old age, sickness, and accident insurance acts, an imperial department of labour—and they had become more cautious as they saw themselves drift within sight of attaining power by constitutional means.

The authoritarian structure of the German state made power a reality for the party that could grasp it, and the Social Democrats were prepared to preserve the system if they could direct it. The basic rift in German political life was a rift between the impotent many and the powerful few; landlords, manufacturers, bankers, bureaucrats, military leaders shaped the national policies in a manner that seemed selfish and monopolistic to the masses. The Social Democrats fought, therefore, to limit great fortunes by imposing inheritance and income taxes, to cut the agrarian profits of the great landowners by lowering the tariff in imported food, to pare the dividends of the corporations and the employers by ensuring higher pay, easier hours, and more favourable working conditions for servants, labourers, and factory hands. They fought, also, to curb the control of the militarists by reducing the annual armament appropriations, for they believed with good reason that the army high command was the citadel of German conservatism. The army had never been democratized; it higher offices were reserved for the Junkers, members of the landed nobility and particularly of the aristocracy of east Prussia. Before 1914, 30 out of 32 commanding generals in the German army, and 37 out of 44 lieutenant-generals, were of noble birth. Against such class favouritism the Social Democrats were pledged to fight. But how were they to democratize the army without weakening it? And might not the officers of the high command prefer to provoke a war, in order to demonstrate their value and capacity, rather than wait until the Social Democratic party climbed to power, curtailed their appropriations, and cancelled their privileges?

In Italy, as in most of Europe, the parties of the Left gained ground in the opening years of the twentieth century. Since the unification of the kingdom two generations earlier, the Chamber of Deputies had contained a Right and a Left grouping, with the leaders of the Right coming as a rule from the industrial north and those of the Left from the south. But this sectional affiliation, and all other distinctions between the rival parties, were of less significance than the fact that both played politics, practised favouritism, and coveted the spoils of office. They alternated in power rather than in policy, and neither maintained a high standard of political honesty or efficiency. From 1896 to 1903 the Right was in power; then the Left forces, dominated by Giovanni Giolitti, took office and controlled Italian politics until the First World War.

Illiteracy, high taxes, low wages, emigration, and lack of essential raw materials such as coal and iron, made it difficult for Italy to play the ambitious role of a great power. Between four and five million Italians sought new homes in North and South America between 1860 and 1914. Unfortunately, those who remained were swayed by an enthusiastic nationalism that easily degenerated into chauvinism. Their political leaders found it convenient to distract popular attention from ills at home by references to *Italia irredenta* (the 'unredeemed' areas including Istria, Trieste, and the Trentino, still held by the Austrians) and to the need for an overseas empire comparable to that of France or

Britain. An attempt to conquer Abyssinia ended in a catastrophic military defeat in 1896. Discontent and lawlessness spread among the impoverished peasants of Naples and Sicily, and syndicalist organizers with a frankly revolutionary programme appealed to the poorly paid industrial workers of Milan and other northern cities. A general strike at Milan (1904) stirred up so much violence that the army was called upon to suppress it.

Imitating the social remedies already initiated by Bismarck in Germany the Italian parliament adopted old age pensions and compulsory insurance against sickness and accidents as early as 1898. Trade unions were legalized, and many public utilities taken over by the municipal or national authorities. But these palliatives failed to relieve the popular discontent or to improve the feeble condition of the national finances. In 1912 the (fourth) Giolitti ministry decided to abolish the literacy and property qualifications limiting the suffrage, and the electorate was expanded from 3,000,000 to 8,500,000 adult males. An election the following year brought a sharp rise in the socialist representation, the number of socialist deputies leaping from forty-one to seventy-eight. It was apparent that in Italy, as in Britain, France, and Germany, the ascendancy of the liberal bourgeoise was threatened by the rising power of the proletariat. But in Italy the Catholic Church, although it was still officially unreconciled with the national government, exerted a powerful restraining influence over the masses and combated the spread of socialist doctrines. In the election of 1913 it was significant that the representation of the Catholic groups rose from fourteen to thirty-five deputies, a larger proportionate increase than that achieved by the socialists.

Spain at the opening of the twentieth century was still in many respects a land of the old régime. The monarch wielded considerable personal power; the Church and the Catholic religious orders retained a privileged position, great wealth, and a decisive influence over education; a few aristocratic families possessed princely domains while landless peasants starved; and the army pursued its own policies, defying the civil government. The army officers knew that their support was indispensable to the king, the debonair but shallow Alphonso XIII. Spanish economic development was slow, with manufacturing, mining, and railway construction largely dependent on foreign capital; and the last relics of the once vast Spanish colonial empire in America and the Philippines were lost to the United States in 1898. Sectionalism, always strong among the Basques and Catalonians, weakened the unity of the nation, while anarchist and syndicalist doctrines spread among the urban workers. Some half-hearted attempts at reform were made between 1898 and 1914, but the clerical question, the land question, the labour question, and the army question continued to resist solution. Spain was obviously drifting towards a social upheaval of unpredictable gravity in which the army, with its preference for military dictatorship, was likely to determine the outcome.

In Portugal parallel conditions prevailed and revo-

lution came more swiftly. Charles I (1889–1908) was
selfish and extravagant; he was assassinated in 1908;
and his successor, Manuel II, was dethroned by a naval
revolt in 1910. Portugal became a republic with a constitution resembling that of France, but apart from some
anti-clerical edicts the new régime did little to change
the basic pattern of Portuguese politics or to improve
the condition of the people. Spain and Portugal together had a population of 26,000,000 in 1914, and the
Portuguese empire in Africa and the East Indies was
twenty times the area of Portugal itself, yet the Iberian
peoples exerted less political, economic, and military
influence in Europe and the world than their history
and their numbers warranted. But despite the severance
of all political ties their linguistic and cultural traditions
still affected the lives of 50,000,000 people in Latin
America, and Spanish remained, after English and
Russian, the most widely spoken of the European
languages.

Belgium and the Netherlands, like Portugal, possessed
overseas empires many times their own area, and like
Portugal they relied upon British friendship and naval
supremacy because without the *pax Britannica* their
possessions would have been highly vulnerable. Belgian
progress in the nineteenth century proved remarkable
and consistent. The constitutional monarchy established after Belgium broke away from the Netherlands
in 1831 functioned smoothly; peace, order, and industrial expansion brought a phenomenal development
of metallurgy and manufacture; and the Belgian population increased to almost 8,000,000 by 1914, making

Belgium the most densely populated country in Europe. The Liberal (bourgeois) party, that controlled Belgian politics from 1849 to 1884, was weakened by the rise of socialism, but the beneficiary of the resulting split was the Catholic party, which achieved parliamentary leadership and controlled the cabinets from 1884 to the First World War. Social legislation, especially after 1900, established old age pensions, legalized trade unions, regulated factory work, and improved the living conditions of the urban classes.

The Netherlands, likewise a constitutional monarchy, had a slightly smaller population than Belgium (6,250,000 in 1914), and Dutch economy was less highly industrialized. Dutch social and political institutions were also less democratic. Until 1887 the electorate did not exceed 150,000; it was doubled in that year, and doubled again in 1896, but it still fell far short of universal suffrage. There was widespread dissatisfaction among the unenfranchised, and minor social reforms did little to allay it. Serious strikes dislocated the railway and shipping services in 1903, and the government, faced with a failure of transport and trade, broke the workers' resistance by calling out the troops. Yet, despite labour troubles at home and repeated insurrections among the native peoples in their populous Indonesian empire, the Netherlanders remained prosperous, ranking fifth in foreign trade and seventh in merchant tonnage among the nations of the world until the outbreak of the First World War.

The Swiss Confederation had an area (16,000 square miles) somewhat larger, and a population (4,000,000) somewhat smaller, than that of the Netherlands in 1914. But Switzerland had no sea-coast, no navy, and no colonies, preserving its independence by prudent diplomacy, with three great powers—Germany, France, and Italy—pressing its frontiers. It lacked many of the characteristics commonly thought essential to a national state: centralization of government, and unity of speech, institutions, and religion. The twenty-two Swiss cantons were sovereign units linked by a loose federal tie. The population was almost evenly divided between the Protestant and Roman Catholic faiths. Two-thirds of the people spoke German, but in five cantons French was the accepted tongue, and in one Italian. Circumspect in their relations with foreigners who visited the Alpine resorts in profitable numbers, vigilant in defence, and industrious in manufacture, commerce, and farming, the Swiss remained peaceful and progressive. A constitution adopted in 1874 provided for universal manhood suffrage, free compulsory education, and religious toleration. In two respects Swiss democracy was the most advanced in Europe by 1914: the electors could demand a plebiscite on any important legislative measure that came before the federal parliament (the referendum), and could initiate legislation on any proposal made by 50,000 or more electors (the initiative).

The smaller countries of Europe, it is interesting to note, tended to conform to a norm or pattern by the beginning of the twentieth century. They had in general about one-eighth of the population and area of the great European powers. They owed their continued existence

as sovereign states less to their own innate capacity for
defence than to the mutual jealousies of strong neighbours, which preserved them from absorption in order
to maintain the European balance of power. This held
true of the three northern states, Denmark, Sweden,
and Norway. The Scandinavian countries, like Switzerland, Belgium, and the Netherlands, occupied an area
of equilibrium equally vital and equally vulnerable to
three powerful neighbours, for Britain, Germany, and
Russia all had interests in the Baltic.

The Scandinavian nations remained at peace throughout the nineteenth century (save for the Danish War of
1864) and evolved along constitutional lines as limited
monarchies, setting an admirable example of political
stability, economic enterprise, and high culture. The
Danes devoted themselves with particular success to
agriculture and dairy farming, the Norwegians built up a
maritime tonnage that ranked fifth in the world by 1914,
and the Swedes developed their machine and metal-
lurgical industries with notable success. The union of
Sweden and Norway under one crown, approved by
the Congress of Vienna, was dissolved peaceably after
almost a century when Norway became an independent
kingdom under a Danish prince in 1905. Norway was
one of the earliest European states to establish woman
suffrage (1907 and 1915); Denmark followed, liberaliz-
ing the voting procedure by constitutional amendments
between 1901 and 1915; and Sweden adopted pro-
portional representation and universal manhood suffrage
after 1907. All three Scandinavian countries lost heavily
by emigration between 1850 and 1914, some 350,000

Danes, 800,000 Norwegians, and 1,500,000 Swedes leaving their homelands during this period.

In contrast to the Baltic nations, with their relatively high literacy, peaceful intercourse, and political stability, the Balkan peoples remained largely illiterate, economically backward, and politically unstable into the twentieth century. The Near Eastern question—the problem of organizing the liberated sections of the Balkan peninsula as the Turkish tide receded, and ultimately the dilemma of deciding which great power would control Constantinople if the Turks were expelled from Europe entirely—had precipitated several acute crises during the nineteenth century. The solution achieved, if it could be considered a solution, was to erect the Balkan provinces into sovereign states as they were successively detached from the sultan's suzerainty. By the opening of the twentieth century three independent kingdoms (Greece, Serbia, and Rumania), and one autonomous but not yet wholly independent kingdom (Bulgaria), had been carved from the shrinking empire of Turkey-in-Europe.

Greece, which had thrown off the Turkish yoke in 1829, was burdened by an excessive foreign debt, insufficient resources, and a rising population (about 2,500,000 in 1900). The kingdom, enlarged by the addition of the Ionian islands in 1864 and Thessaly in 1881, had an area of almost 25,000 square miles, which was increased to 28,000 in 1913 by the annexation of Crete. The poverty prevailing among the peasant population and dislike of military service prompted some 15,000 Greeks to emigrate annually after 1900.

Serbia, which likewise had a population of about 2,500,000 in 1900, was at that date an inland kingdom of 19,000 square miles. Guaranteed autonomy in 1829, the Serbs forced the withdrawal of the last Turk garrisons in 1867 and became entirely independent in 1878. Serbia was constantly shaken by the plots of pro-Austrian and pro-Russian factions; the arbitrary rule of Alexander I (1889–1903) ended in his assassination; and his successor Peter I, of the rival Karageorge dynasty, linked Serbian policies with those of Russia, stimulating the Pan-Slav hostility towards Austria that already agitated the Serb people.

Rumania was the largest and most populous of the Balkan states when the twentieth century opened, a country exceeding 50,000 square miles in area, with 6,000,000 inhabitants. Formed from the Danubian principalities, Moldavia and Wallachia, when these became autonomous (1861), Rumania was recognized as independent in 1878, losing Bessarabia to Russia while gaining the Dobruja in exchange. The Rumanians were more Latin than Slavonic, and considered themselves descendants of Roman colonists who settled in ancient Dacia.

Below Rumania and south of the Danube lay the kingdom of Bulgaria, with an area of 37,000 square miles and 4,000,000 people. The congress of Berlin set up autonomous principalities of Bulgaria and eastern Rumelia in 1878, and these were united seven years later. The Bulgars did not assert their complete independence from Turkey until 1908.

Balkan politics could not well be tranquillized while

Austrian and Russian agents strove to manipulate the unstable régimes and utilize the factional feuds to promote policies devised at Vienna and St Petersburg. Half the inhabitants of the Austro-Hungarian empire were Slavs; they were dissatisfied because they were exploited economically and politically by the dominant German and Magyar groups; and they were susceptible to Pan-Slav propaganda calling for the formation of a Slav bloc in south-eastern Europe. This threat kept the Austrian and Hungarian statesmen in a state of nervous apprehension, but they hesitated to mollify the Slav subjects of Francis Joseph by democratic reforms and concessions, and could only oppose a blind opposition to the expansionist dreams of the Balkan nations, especially the Serbs. The Habsburg empire was a weakening anachronism, but it had the support of Germany, the leading military power of Europe, and could thus assume the risk of defying Slav agitation and Russian pressure.

The Russian government, in the opening decade of the twentieth century, had difficulties and distractions of its own. The impact of the industrial and technological revolutions struck Russian society while it was still in many respects half-feudal and half-medieval. An energetic reformer, Serge Witte, recognized the disadvantages under which Russia laboured because of its retarded economy: as late as 1913 Russian foreign trade was less than that of Belgium, although Russia had twenty times the population and six hundred times the area of that small but highly industrialized state. Witte became minister of finance in 1893, and laboured for ten years to expand Russian factories, railways, mines, arsenals, shipyards, and banks, in order to make the Tsar's empire capable of sustaining the role of a great power in peace and war. But his policies were attacked by the Slavophils, who feared western influences, and when Witte appealed to the zemstvos (provincial assemblies) in 1902 a majority of the replies criticized his economic policies. Tsar Nicholas II thereupon removed him from office, ignoring the fact that the criticism had been levelled even more directly against the autocratic political system that denied Russia a national parliament and a responsible ministry.

There was justice, however, in the claim of the conservatives that the progress of industry, which Witte had fostered, increased the opposition to the Tsar's régime. The urban workers, collecting in the expanding factory towns, organized labour unions and adopted revolutionary slogans. Russia was still a predominantly agricultural country, but industrial workers could be organized much more effectively than peasants, and by 1914 one-seventh of the population had gathered into the cities. Witte had planned to placate this rising proletariat with social legislation, promising accident insurance, pensions, and similar benefits, but the discontent increased after his dismissal. Economic progress also strengthened the Russian bourgeoisie, hitherto limited in numbers and without political power, and the business classes favoured liberal reforms in government and a system of national representation.

Thus the dangers of revolution rose rapidly in Russia after 1900. The peasants had long been discontented;

P

the intellectuals were persistently critical; the small middle class envied the parliamentary influence which their class commanded in western Europe; the workers, increasingly class-conscious and aggressive, read Marxist pamphlets and preached socialism. Finally, the subject nationalities of the Tsar, the Finns and Poles in particular, were antagonized by the policy of 'Russification' whereby the Slavophils and nationalists strove to extend the Russian language and Orthodox religion throughout the empire. So long as the revolutionary factions remained weak and divided the secret police found it possible to repress them; anarchism and terrorism had been sternly checked after Alexander II was assassinated in 1881. But no police force could cope with the class movements and rising social pressures that developed after 1900. The ancient formula of Orthodoxy, Autocracy, Nationalism, was losing its appeal as the pervasive influences generated by liberalism and industrialism leavened Russian society. Any reverse that exposed the lethargy and inefficiency of the bureaucracy to public condemnation, and focused the widening discontent on the officials responsible, was certain to produce a crisis for the régime.

The crisis came in 1905 after military and naval disasters in the Far East had revealed the extent of Russian unpreparedness and incapacity. How the Russo-Japanese War tilted the international balance of power will be discussed later. Its effect upon the internal balance in Russia itself, already so precarious, was to stir up a popular outbust that came as near to overturning the régime as a revolution can come without succeeding. The hated minister of the interior, Viacheslav Plehve, was assassinated; workers who attempted peacefully to petition the Tsar were repulsed with volleys that killed seventy (Bloody Sunday, 22 January 1905); the St. Petersburg unions organized soviets to direct the popular movement; and Nicholas II realized that until he could recall his best troops from Manchuria he must make concessions or lose his throne. Dismissing his reactionary advisers, he restored Witte to favour and promised a constitution and a popular national assembly, with guarantees of civil liberties (October Manifesto, 1905).

This capitulation satisfied the moderates who believed the Tsar would keep his promises. The more progressive liberals organized the Constitutional Democratic party and demanded a constituent assembly, while the Social Democrats and radical working men rejected the Tsar's programme entirely. But the October Manifesto served its purpose. It postponed the crisis and it split the ranks of the opposition. Throughout the winter of 1905–6 the military forces returned from Manchuria, to repress the working-class demonstrations in St. Petersburg with much bloodshed and to restore order in the provinces. Witte secured large loans from France and Britain (the French had a military alliance with the Russian government and wanted to maintain it), and this financial aid tided the Tsarist régime over its crisis. When the promised assembly (the Duma) met in May 1906, Nicholas II was in a sufficiently strong position to chasten it, and to insist that the promises he had made in his October Manifesto assured the Russian people a national parliament but did not compromise the absolute powers he had inherited.

This first Duma had been elected by what amounted to universal manhood suffrage, but the radical parties had declined to participate and the Constitutional Democrats (Cadets) emerged with the largest representation. Even they were bitterly disappointed, for the 'Octobrists' who had placed their faith in Nicholas found that he did not wait for the Duma to meet but issued a set of fundamental laws for the empire on his own initiative. When the deputies of the nation criticized them as insufficient he dismissed the Duma for its contumacy. The more audacious members adjourned to Viborg in Finland and drafted a manifesto urging the Russian people to refuse taxes until their liberties were assured, but the gesture aroused slight response. A second Duma, elected in 1907, proved even more recalcitrant than the first. Nicholas therefore revised the franchise, increasing the representation of the propertied groups while decreasing that of the workers and peasants: the result, not surprisingly, was a third Duma more amenable to his wishes.

Russian autocracy had survived the most critical test it had yet faced. From 1907 until the First World War there was an uneasy political truce while the reactionaries congratulated themselves on the Tsar's firmness and the revolutionaries analysed their mistakes. Some cautious reforms were attempted in social legislation and education, economic progress continued, and the compromise with autocracy represented by a legislative assembly that could not legislate served its anomalous purpose. In Peter Stolypin the Tsar found a minister with the character and skill to manage the tamed Duma, but Stolypin was assassinated in 1911. A fourth Duma, elected in 1912, discussed but failed to attack the vital issues—the land question, the labour question, a responsible ministry, the energetic development of Russian resources—and it was still in session when Russia was engulfed in the First World War. The moment was approaching when military defeats would unleash a revolution that could not be held in check, a revolution that Tsardom could not survive.

In the new world of the Americas the United States was the only country that had developed an industrial economy to match that of Europe. There too, by 1900, mushroom cities had drawn men from the forest and the farm to the mill and the workshop. In the first decade of the twentieth century American economic expansion rapidly quickened its pace, and the phenomenal gains which it made showed the unlimited productive capacity of American factories. Iron production rose 50 per cent. within ten years; coal production doubled; oil production trebled. As in Europe, the expanding industries tended to amalgamate, and corporations or 'trusts' took shape, dominating and in some cases almost monopolizing an entire field of manufacture, mining, or transportation. Steel trusts, oil trusts, and electric power trusts were followed by combinations to control a single raw commodity, such as copper, lead or coal, or to 'corner' the market by organizing the facilities that went to a single item of merchandise such as plate glass or wire nails. Even before 1900 this concentration in manufacturing, transportation, and finance had proceeded so rapidly that it threatened to nullify the system of free economic enterprise. Great millionaire corporations, with their headquarters in the eastern cities, became so powerful, and in some cases so unscrupulous, that they bought out or made bankrupt lesser competitors. Subsidiary enterprises were absorbed by securing 51 per cent. of their stock, and a small number of financiers and industrialists could acquire vast influence through interlocking directorates whereby they determined the policies of several companies operating in allied enterprises. The growth and centralization of power through business combinations advanced so swiftly that the United States had already surpassed Great Britain, France, and Germany in this respect when the twentieth century opened.

In the organization of labour, on the other hand, the United States lagged behind the leading European countries. The American Federation of Labour, formed in 1886 with 150,000 members, increased its membership to almost 3,000,000 by 1914, but it lacked political power and representation. The division of political authority between the state legislatures and the federal Congress made it difficult to adopt any uniform and far-reaching programme of labour legislation. Laws passed in one state to raise wage rates or limit profits might defeat their aims by driving manufacturers to move their factories or incorporate their companies in another state where the laws were more favourable to them. Only a federal act that could be enforced throughout the nation was likely to provide a charter for labour, but even federal acts could miscarry. In 1890, for instance, the Congress enacted an Anti-Trust Law which declared illegal 'every contract, combination in the form of trust or otherwise, or conspiracy in restraint of trade or commerce among the several states or with foreign nations'. This loose wording left the interpretation of the act to the courts which ruled (1895) that it forbade labour union leaders to call a strike if this involved 'restraint of interstate commerce'. Yet two years later, when the question arose whether the act applied to mergers or combinations of railway companies, the court ruled that it did not. Labour leaders became convinced, not without reason, that organized justice, or at least the interpretation of the statutes, favoured 'Big Business'. They continued to work for remedial legislation, shorter hours, higher pay, safety devices in mines and factories, and compensation for workmen injured at their trade, but the progress made was slow and unsatisfactory.

One reason for this delay was the absence in the United States of an active and effective socialist party, to match the Labour party in Great Britain and the united socialist groups in France and Germany. Although an American socialist party was organized in 1901, it did not play a significant role in politics until the election of 1912, when its candidates obtained almost one million votes. Even this defection from the ranks of the two established parties, the Republicans and the Democrats, could not be interpreted as a real revolt of American labour. There was, it is true, a widespread dissatisfaction with the 'Big Business' interests and their monopolistic methods, and an equally wide criticism of American foreign policy, which had taken an imperialist turn after 1900. But the swing towards the left, discernible in the American elections of 1910 and 1912, was much less vehement than the leftward trend in European politics that marked the decade before 1914.

From the foundation of the republic the electors in the United States had shown a strong preference for the two-party system. The Northern victory in the Civil War left the Republican party in the saddle, and from 1865 to 1900 the Democratic party won only two presidential elections. In 1900 a Republican victory placed William McKinley in the White House; his assassination in 1901 brought the Vice-President, Theodore Roosevelt, into office. Roosevelt was energetic, popular, and progressive. He was re-elected in 1904, and in 1908 the Republicans won again, placing William Howard Taft in power as 26th President. But signs of defection and opposition were appearing within and without the Republican ranks. In the election of 1910 the Democrats secured a majority in the House of Representatives. The electors had grown increasingly critical of the 'Old Guard' leadership of the Republican party; it was attacked on the ground that it had proved too lenient towards the trusts, had maintained an excessively high tariff, and had pursued an aggressive policy of interference in Latin America. When Taft was nominated for re-election in 1912 Roosevelt split the Republican organization and ran as candidate of a 'Progressive' insurgent group, bidding for popular support by advocating more explicit anti-trust laws, abolition of child labour, and similar reforms. But the Republicans, even 'progressive' Republicans, were identified in the public mind with business interests, and the Democratic candidate, Woodrow Wilson, won the three-cornered election.

Wilson believed that he had a popular mandate to carry through a programme of domestic reforms. He created a Department of Labour, approved a reduction in the tariff rates, and increased public control over the banking system. An amendment to the Constitution (1913) empowered Congress to levy a federal income tax. A stricter law on combinations (Clayton Anti-Trust Act) curbed monopolistic practices in business, prohibited interlocking directorates in large corporations, and specifically excepted labour unions from its provisions, reversing the court decision of 1895. After 1914 friction with Mexico and increasing involvements arising from the war in Europe partly diverted Wilson's attention from domestic affairs, and the strength of the Democratic following declined. But the Democrats had now identified themselves with a policy of social reform. This was highly significant for the future, because the trend of the age was towards political control of the national economy and social legislation to improve the condition of the common man. The half-century in American history that preceded Wilson's victory in 1912 had been a period of Republican ascendancy with business expanding freely under a minimum of control; the period that followed 1912 was to see the Democrats in power for the greater part of the time with increasing federal control over business activities. The social and economic life of the nation was to be increasingly regimented in peace and war to a degree that most nineteenth-century Americans would have found almost inconceivable.

In British North America the opening years of the twentieth century brought mounting waves of immigration and rapid expansion in the central and western regions of the dominion. The provinces of Alberta and Saskatchewan were admitted (1905) and a second transcontinental railway completed in 1914. Canada sent two contingents to fight with the British in the South African War, but the Canadian Senate rejected a bill to contribute three Dreadnoughts to the imperial navy (1913). Economic and financial ties with the mother country remained close; a preferential tariff with Britain was adopted in 1898, while a treaty for trade reciprocity with the United States was opposed by a majority of the Canadian electors in 1911.

In Latin America the history of the various republics continued to follow the pattern set in the nineteenth century; no profound changes marked the years from 1898 to 1914. A revolution in Mexico (1911) opened a period of disorder and civil war. The government of Colombia failed to grant the United States permission to build a canal across the isthmus of Panama (1903), whereupon the province of Panama seceded from Colombia, was promptly recognized by the United States as an independent republic, and granted the lease desired. The canal was completed in 1914. But the high-handed methods adopted by the United States

government, which landed armed forces to maintain
order in Cuba, the Dominican Republic, Haiti, Nicara-
gua, and at other points in Central America and the
Caribbean, aroused opposition among Latin Americans
against the 'Colossus of the North'. Inter-American relations were strained and unsatisfactory in the years
preceding the First World War, but efforts were made
to improve them. Occasional congresses called to promote friendly understandings and arbitrate disputes led
to the formal creation (1910) of the Pan-American
Union, an agency of conciliation which included
the diplomatic representatives of all the American
republics.

The southern hemisphere, which had hitherto supported only an insignificant fraction of the population
of the globe, began to play a more impressive part in
world affairs by the opening of the twentieth century.
In the Argentine Republic a population of 1,700,000
(1869) was multiplied fivefold in half a century to reach
9,000,000 by the First World War, largely through the
influx of Spanish and Italian immigrants. The Union
of South Africa, created in 1909, had over a million
inhabitants of European descent. In the South Pacific
the Commonwealth of Australia, proclaimed in 1901,
had a population of four millions by 1914, almost exclusively of European blood; while New Zealand, which
acquired dominion status in 1907, contained a million
white settlers by that date. The determination of the
Australians and New Zealanders to preserve white
supremacy led them to exclude immigrants who came
from the more densely populated continents of Asia

and Africa, and they were prepared to enforce this determination by arms if necessary. Australia established the nucleus of a navy in 1908 and adopted military conscription in 1911; New Zealand likewise provided for universal military training and contributed to the support of the British fleet.

From these new dominions rising to nationhood in the Antipodes, attention must now be turned back to Europe itself. During the two decades before 1914 a fateful game was played out on the European chessboard, a game that seems in retrospect one of the most deadly tournaments ever waged by Old World diplomats. It is important to recall again that the successive decisions on international problems taken between 1894 and 1914 were often manœuvres of the moment. No one could foretell how firmly the alliances then formed would work, nor predict that they would hold fast under strain. Yet the trend of international events had its own inexorable logic, dividing Europe more and more definitely into two opposing camps. The balance of power, invoked by statesmen as the surest guarantee of peace, became instead a mechanism so delicately interlocked that it made almost inevitable (as an alternative to general peace) a general war. The diplomatic history of the period from 1894 to 1914 is the story of how the six great powers of Europe came to be ranged in two rival systems of alliances, with the tension between the systems growing until it became unendurable.

From the date of its proclamation in 1871 the German empire was the leading military state of Europe. Bismarck was haunted by the fear that German security might be threatened by a coalition of powers; he was persuaded that France would be the logical core of such a coalition; and he worked for twenty years to keep France diplomatically isolated. His agreements with Austria and Italy (the Triple Alliance) and his understanding with Austria and Russia (the Three Emperors' League), so long as they remained in effect, left France no important continental ally. But Bismarck's dismissal in 1890 was followed by the decline and ultimately by the collapse of his system. In 1890 the German foreign office decided not to renew the Reinsurance treaty with Russia; this agreement had been made, in 1887, because Russia declined to prolong the Three Emperors' League, and it provided primarily that neither power would join in an attack against the other. The Russians were willing to renew this guarantee, and the attitude of the German foreign office puzzled and alarmed them. Prompt French overtures to St. Petersburg for a Franco-Russian military alliance had little result at the moment, but the French were persistent. Early in 1894 a convention was concluded binding France to aid Russia and Russia to aid France if either were attacked by Germany. This new agreement was to remain in force as long as the Triple Alliance endured, an admission that it was intended as a counterweight to the understanding then uniting Germany, Austria, and Italy. But the Franco-Russia convention had a second purpose. Both members were competing with Great Britain at a number of points, the French in North Africa and south-east Asia, the Russians in the Near East, Persia, and Afghanistan. As France and Russia had no sharp conflict of aims at any point, they could afford to strengthen one another in resisting British pressure.

In London the Franco-Russian pact aroused misgivings, and relations between Britain and France remained fretful until they reached a crisis in 1898. The discovery that a French expedition from Equatorial Africa had penetrated to the valley of the upper Nile at Fashoda brought both powers close to a state of war until the French withdrew their outpost. This peaceful solution was fostered by the new French foreign minister, Théophile Delcassé, whose seven years of service in that office were to be largely devoted to cementing an Anglo-French accord. At the moment the British were still satisfied with their 'splendid isolation', but their attitude changed steadily in the next few years. The South African War brought home to them the cost of military unpreparedness. The death of Queen Victoria in 1901 and the retirement of Salisbury in the next year were followed by a change of mood in British diplomacy. Edward VII distrusted his nephew, William II, and was sympathetic towards the French. But a much more powerful factor in changing the British attitude was the German naval programme. Commencing in 1898 the Germans undertook the construction of a High Seas Fleet, and on New Year's Day 1900 the Kaiser announced his intention of making the German navy equal to the German army. At the same time the minister of marine, Admiral Alfred von Tirpitz, revealed the conviction behind this naval programme by uttering a significant prophecy. 'In the coming century', he warned, 'the German people must be either the hammer or the anvil.'

The boasts of indiscreet German writers and the information compiled by the British naval intelligence agents strengthened the belief in England that Germany rather than France or Russia would prove the chief threat to British naval security in the foreseeable future. German plans called for the launching of fourteen battleships between 1900 and 1905, with twelve more laid down, a rate of building that would make Germany the second naval power of the world by 1906. German naval strength, moreover, could be concentrated in the North Sea while British warships were scattered throughout the oceans of the globe. That the British admiralty recognized the threat which this implied is clear from the measures adopted after 1902. By an understanding negotiated with Japan in that year Britain and Japan agreed that both would maintain in the Far East 'a naval force superior in strength to that of any third power'. The basic fact in this Anglo-Japanese accord was that it ruled out the danger of a Russo-Japanese alliance which would have placed the British Far Eastern squadron in grave danger. Britain was seeking to minimize the risk of a hostile combination in that distant area so that new ships under construction might be kept at home.

The second major move the British made to concentrate their navy in home waters came in 1904. Anglo-French relations had been improving steadily for two years; the differences between the two powers in Africa were smoothed away by an agreement that left

Egypt a sphere of British influence while France acquired paramount control in Morocco; and this happy reconciliation was celebrated by the conclusion of the *Entente Cordiale* in 1904. The *Entente* was not a treaty of alliance, but it established a friendly understanding, and it left the British reasonably confident that they need not fear an attack by the French in the Mediterranean. It had the further advantage that it reduced the danger of a Franco-Russian war against Britain, and thus left the admiralty in London free to turn its main attention to the growing threat presented by the German High Seas Fleet at Kiel. The first specific British plans for the disposition of torpedo craft in the event of a war with Germany were issued in the summer of 1904.

Meanwhile developments in the Far East were changing the precarious balance of power in a manner at once swift and unforeseen. On 4 February 1904 the Japanese made a sudden attack on the Russian naval base at Port Arthur, bottling up the Russian Far Eastern fleet. Japanese armies were landed to besiege the port and a large-scale war developed as the Russians brought up reinforcements. The initiative and energy of the Japanese astonished European observers, and the astonishment mounted as the Japanese compelled Port Arthur to capitulate after a year's siege and defeated a second Russian army at Mukden. With command of the sea the Japanese could supply their forces readily, while the Russians had to fight at the end of the Trans-Siberian railway. A struggle waged so far away did not involve any other European powers directly. But the fact that France was the tacit ally of Russia and Britain of Japan made both nations aware of the advantage Germany would derive if they became involved. This realization helped to stimulate the *Entente* reached by France and Britain shortly after the outbreak of hostilities in the Far East. Germany, meanwhile, displayed a friendly neutrality towards Russia, and the Kaiser went so far as to promise the Tsar that Russia could count upon German aid if Britain went to the assistance of the Japanese.

The Japanese, however, were doing very well by themselves. With internal revolts crippling the Russian war effort, the Tsar's government played its last card by sending the Russian Baltic fleet to Far Eastern waters to re-establish naval control; it reached the Straits of Tsushima in May 1905, and was totally destroyed by the Japanese. Not since the Battle of Trafalgar one hundred years earlier had the world seen such an overwhelming naval disaster. The Russians had now lost every battle in this one-sided war. They made peace in September 1905, at Portsmouth, New Hampshire, after President Theodore Roosevelt had offered his mediation to hasten this result. Russian and Japanese forces were withdrawn from Manchuria which was restored to China, but the Japanese won virtual possession of Korea, annexed the southern half of Sakhalin island, and took over the Russian lease of the Liaotung peninsula.

The threat of revolution within Russia made peace a necessity for the Tsar's harassed government. Had the war continued the outcome might have been less unequal, since the Russians had built up an army of a

Q

million men in Manchuria, the Japanese lines were widely extended, and the financial strain of a major conflict was exhausting Japanese resources. There was bitter disappointment in Tokyo because the peace terms failed to include a financial indemnity.

In Europe the revelation of Russian weakness set up a dangerous oscillation in the balance of power. The French, with their one certain ally temporarily enfeebled, felt themselves gravely threatened by the might of Germany. In Berlin the fear of a two-front war dissolved as it became evident that Russia would require several years for recovery. The advisers who surrounded William II believed the moment ripe for Germany to take a bold stand, to extort concessions from France in the colonial field and to press the Austro-German drive in the Near East. From 1905 to 1914 the tension in Europe was to mount steadily and the issues that revealed this tension may be summarized under three heads, the colonial question, the naval question, and the Balkan question.

The first German move, undertaken in 1905, involved the colonial question and might be described as exploratory. It was designed to test the reality of the Anglo-French *Entente*. The French received a sharp warning from Berlin that German interests in Morocco had been ignored and compensation must be provided. Delcassé put his trust in British support and wished to defy the German threat. But his colleagues in the French cabinet lacked his confidence; Delcassé was forced to resign the post of foreign minister which he had filled for seven years; and France yielded to the German demands for an international conference on the Moroccan problem. Diplomatic representatives of all the great powers met at Algeciras in January 1906, but only the Austrians supported the German stand. The conference declared Morocco an independent sultanate; but it also recognized the right of the French to exercise 'police power' in the area. This ambiguous concession left the way open for further expansion of French influence, which continued to spread (as German diplomats noted) 'like an oil stain'.

Algeciras marked a rebuff for Germany. Even the Italians failed to stand by the Triple Alliance, for Delcassé succeeded before his fall in reconciling French and Italian conflicts in the Mediterranean. Instead of weakening the Anglo-French *Entente* the dispute over Morocco strengthened it. While the conference was still in session French and British military experts discussed secret plans for landing 100,000 British troops in France if war came.

In reality colonial disputes were less dangerous than they appeared, chiefly because no colonial issue could affect the vital interests of all the great powers. Russia was not likely to risk war to support French claims in the Congo, nor Austria to mobilize for the defence of German trade in Morocco. This fact helps to explain why the Moroccan difficulties were settled peaceably not once but three times. In 1908 a second dispute arose there when the French seized three German deserters from their foreign legion, invading the German consulate at Casablanca to arrest the fugitives. This 'Casablanca Affair' was submitted to a board of arbitration.

In 1911, when French troops in Morocco marched into Fez, the Germans protested again. But Britain stood behind France; the crisis passed; and France emerged with a virtual protectorate over Morocco, buying Germany off with the cession of 100,000 square miles of the French Congo.

The Anglo-French *Entente* had grown stronger under strain. From 1906 to 1909 French policy was directed by the resolute and irascible Georges Clemenceau, who maintained Delcassé's policy of co-operation with Britain. Furthermore, British distrust of Russia was largely dissipated by the outcome of the Russo-Japanese War, and Clemenceau's mediation hastened an Anglo-Russian accord concluded in 1907. Rivalry between the two powers in the Middle East was reduced by establishing joint spheres of influence in Persia, while Russia recognized the preponderant interest of the British in the Persian Gulf and Afghanistan. No formal alliance yet bound Britain, France, and Russia, but they were clearly drawing together. The revival of Russia as a military power was hastened by the French government, which authorized loans of several thousand millions of francs to aid the Tsar and hasten Russian rearmament. The years 1906–7 thus brought the first clear indication that Europe was dividing into two major systems of alliances with three great powers on each side: a Triple *Entente* was coming into being to offset the weight of the Triple Alliance.

These same years 1906–7 saw the second major issue, the naval question, take a more acute form, for Britain launched the first Dreadnought in 1906. The revolutionary features of this new capital ship rendered all existing navies (including the British) obsolete. As late as 1900 effective battle-range was considered to be about 2,000 yards, or a little more than one mile. In reality the invention of smokeless powder, improved fire control, and more accurate range-finders made effective action possible at four or five times that distance. British naval experts had been pondering these new possibilities when the Russo-Japanese War provided practical demonstrations of long-range firing. Their answer was the Dreadnought, which was protected by eleven-inch armour, carried ten twelve-inch guns, and was equipped with turbine engines that gave it a speed of twenty-one knots. It was better protected, faster, and twice as heavily armed as any warship then afloat, and its appearance opened a new epoch in naval competition. Architects and strategists grasped the costly truth that the war fleets of the world would have to be rebuilt, and in this new race the British were only one year ahead because the Dreadnought had been constructed in twelve months. Only a general agreement among the leading powers to limit their building programmes could avert a deadly and extravagant race. But, despite talks on naval limitation at the Hague Peace Conference in 1907, at a London Naval Conference in 1908, and at Berlin in 1912, no solution acceptable to both the Germans and the British could be found. Without such an accord, Britain and Germany, as the leading sea powers of the world, were condemned to watch one another's naval appropriations and outbid them. It was this naval rivalry, more than any other factor, that focused British attention on Germany as the predestined foe.

The third international issue noted above, the Balkan question, was less clear-cut but even more hazardous. All the great powers were interested in the affairs of the Near East, and for the Austrians and Russians the Balkan peninsula and the Straits were vital areas. Austro-German influence there had been growing since 1900; and in 1908 Austria stole a march by annexing Bosnia and Herzegovina, still nominally part of the sultan's empire, but under Austrian administration since the Congress of Berlin of 1878. Russian protests proved ineffectual, and the Serbs, who were ready to start a war over this Austrian absorption of their fellow Slavs, were warned to keep the peace. The Balkan crisis of 1908 passed because neither France nor Britain was ready to back Russia in meeting the Austrian coup. But there was grave anxiety at Paris and London over the *Drang nach Osten*, the Austro-German drive to the east. The construction of a railroad through the Balkans to Constantinople and thence to Bagdad promised to draw Turkey and the Persian Gulf within the range of German imperialism. Neither Britain nor Russia could permit Constantinople and the Straits to pass under German control, and France likewise had interests to guard in the Levant.

The Ottoman empire was ready to fall apart and no plans had been concerted by the powers for a peaceful division of the sultan's legacy. The British had already occupied Egypt; the French were established in Algeria, Tunis, and Morocco. In 1911 the Italians invaded Tripoli and annexed it; they had bargained for French and British acquiescence by tacit promises not to stand by the Triple Alliance in the event of a general war, and had then won the consent of the Germans and Austrians for their venture by renewing the alliance before it expired. For a year the Ottoman government at Constantinople refused to admit the loss of Tripoli, but events forced it to conclude peace with Italy in October 1912. A new danger had arisen. The evident weakness of Turkey had inspired the Balkan states, Serbia, Greece, and Bulgaria, to open an attack on the sultan's empire, with the proud announcement that they intended to drive the Turks from their last foothold in Europe.

This First Balkan War of 1912 brought speedy victories to the allies; Serbian forces overran most of Albania while the Bulgarians advanced on Constantinople. Then the great powers called a halt. Austria would not permit the Serbs to keep Albania, Russia opposed the Bulgarian claims to Thrace. A temporary settlement, worked out at London in May 1913, broke down immediately because Bulgaria attacked its late ally, Serbia, and was attacked in turn by Greece, Rumania, and Turkey. Within a few months Bulgaria was stripped of almost all its recent gains. The great powers, intervening once again, forced the Serbs and Greeks to abandon Albania, which was set up as an independent principality. Austrian opposition had been thrown into the scale against the creation of a greater Serbia, with an outlet on the Adriatic Sea, because the Austrian government was insecure. Half the inhabitants of the Habsburg empire were Slavs; many of them were discontented; and the emergence of a Pan-Slav state or a Slav Confederation in the Balkans would, it was feared, dissolve the crumbling frontiers of the Austro-Hungarian realm. The Pan-Slav dream, with Russia in the background, was a nightmare to the diplomats at Vienna and Budapest.

Around the Balkan cockpit, like gamblers that have staked more than they can afford to lose on their favourites, the great powers watched and wrangled through the struggles of 1912 and 1913. With each shift in fortune the odds increased; the ledgers of Europe told the story of these final years of tension with bleak impersonality. Since 1871 the European peoples had been living under an 'armed peace' that grew more costly to maintain with each passing decade. Military and naval expenditures doubled between 1880 and 1900, then doubled again between 1900 and 1910. For the sixteen-year period from 1898 to 1914—the period covered in this chapter—the annual armament bill of the great powers rose 140 per cent. Standing armies were increased after every crisis, and Germany, as the leading military power, set the pace. When France and Russia became allies in 1894 German forces were raised from 487,000 to 557,000. When France and Britain established their *Entente* in 1904 the German standing army rose to 605,000. In 1910 it was 617,000; in 1911, 631,000; in 1912, 666,000; in 1913, 761,000; in 1914, 820,000. The French countered in 1913 by extending the period of military service, and the peace-time strength of their army was advanced to 750,000. Russia followed the trend the same year by planning an increase in effectives from 1,300,000 to 1,800,000 men. Great Britain, without a system of military conscription, had less than 300,000 men in the regular army, and of these 110,000 were stationed in the colonies and protectorates. In addition, there was a volunteer force, the Territorials, the members of which had received short periods of training and could be mobilized for national defence. This was a small army for a great power, but the British placed their trust in the Royal Navy as the shield of their empire and their island.

On the sea the *Entente* nations, Britain, France, and Russia, held an unquestionable superiority. The Russian navy was the least powerful of the three and could undertake only local defence in the Baltic and Black Sea. The French battleships, by agreement with the British, were concentrated in the Mediterranean, where they could outmatch any likely combination of Austrian and Italian forces. In the North Sea the British Grand Fleet faced the German High Seas Fleet with a decisive margin in all major categories. The British had sixty-four battleships against forty, ten battle cruisers to four, and a two-to-one advantage in light cruisers, torpedo-boats, and destroyers.

The German bid for naval power, opened in 1898, had produced the second most powerful navy in the world by 1914. But the British had strained their resources to maintain their ascendancy, and they could face the German challenge with confidence. If war came between the Triple Alliance and the Triple *Entente*, the *Entente* powers could control the seas of the world with British aid. But could they count on British

Q*

aid? No formal treaty bound Britain to France or
Russia; yet the French had left their North Sea coast
almost undefended by an agreement with Britain which
assumed that the British navy would defend it. These
naval agreements, and the disposition of the French and
British fleets, were based upon the reality of an Anglo-
French alliance; it was the denial that such an alliance
existed which constituted a fiction. The British people
still preferred to believe that, if a general war developed
on the continent, they were at liberty to proclaim their
neutrality, but their neutrality was already compromised
almost beyond redemption.

By 1914 all the diplomats knew that 'peace was at
the mercy of an accident'. The implications of the
interlocking alliances, the irreversible momentum that
would be released the moment the great powers mobilized, were clear to the generals and the statesmen.
Mobilization, they reminded one another fatalistic-
ally, meant war. But forty years of general peace in
Europe had lulled the peoples into a false dream of
security; they went about their affairs in happy ignor-
ance while the anvil chorus quickened and the continent
echoed to the march of armed millions engaged in their
annual manœuvres. Each year produced its diplomatic
crisis; each year the foreign ministers blustered and
dissembled and compromised; each year the crisis
passed. The diplomats knew how closely they were
circling the maelstrom of war, but they were caught in
the current and they had no policy that looked beyond
the moment. They grappled with each emergency as it
arose, improvising solutions while time ran out and the

hour approached when no new solution could be improvised.

On 28 June 1914 the Archduke Franz Ferdinand, nephew of the Emperor Francis Joseph and heir to the Austrian throne, was shot while on a tour of inspection in Sarajevo, Bosnia. The assassin was a Bosnian youth who had obtained weapons and aid from the Serbian 'Union or Death' society, a terrorist organization formed to agitate against Austria. Officers in the Serbian bureau of military intelligence had encouraged the plot and rumours of it had reached some Serbian cabinet members who failed to counteract it or to warn the Austrian government. Convinced that Serbian officials were implicated, although satisfactory proof of this was not yet in their hands, the statesmen at Vienna determined to teach the Serbs a lesson that would humble them and discourage further plotting. After waiting four weeks to complete its preparations and obtain an assurance from Berlin that Germany would stand firmly behind it, the Austro-Hungarian government presented an ultimatum to Serbia on 23 July. The Serbs accepted most of the conditions within the forty-eight hours allowed them, but simultaneously they began mobilization. Russia supported them, France supported Russia, and ten days later Europe was at war. The crisis for which no peaceful solution could be improvised had arrived.

NOTE ON FURTHER READING

THREE volumes (X–XII) of *The Cambridge Modern History* (Cambridge and New York, 1902–12) deal with Europe after 1815. A reprint, with the bibliographies omitted, was issued in 1934. This valuable and authoritative work is now yielding priority to *The New Cambridge Modern History*, with twelve volumes of text (Cambridge and New York, 1957 ff.). *The Rise of Modern Europe* (New York, 1934 ff.), planned in twenty volumes, has five (13–17) devoted to the century 1814–1914. These sets cover the general history of Europe from the close of the Middle Ages. *The Oxford History of Modern Europe* (Oxford and New York, 1954 ff.) is designed to treat all important aspects of European history for a shorter time span, 1789–1945, in sixteen volumes. The first to appear, *The Struggle for Mastery in Europe, 1848–1918*, by A. J. P. Taylor, was published in 1954.

Most of these works include relevant bibliographies but *The New Cambridge Modern History* reserves them for a separate volume. There is a convenient *Select List of Books on European History, 1815–1914* compiled by A. L. C. Bullock and A. J. P. Taylor (Oxford, 1949; 2nd edition, 1957). Readers who wish for critical estimates of new and significant works on the period as they appear will find them discussed in *The English Historical Review*, in *History*, and frequently in *The Times Literary Supplement*. For American readers similar information may be sought in *The American Historical Review* and *The Journal of Modern History*.

One of the most useful and widely available historical atlases, with some fifty maps on nineteenth-century developments, is that provided to accompany the original *Cambridge Modern History* (1912; 2nd edition, 1926).

Articles in the better encyclopaedias on the countries, institutions, wars, and major historical figures of nineteenth-century Europe commonly include brief mention of the most important sources and secondary works on the subject discussed. For a yearly chronicle of events and contemporary judgements on them the *Annual Register* (continued from 1758 to the present time) is diversified and illuminating. Its information may be supplemented, for the later nineteenth century, by the factual and statistical data to be found in the annual volumes of *The Statesman's Year-Book* (London and New York, from 1864).

INDEX

Dates of monarchs are those of the years during which they reigned; dates of other persons are those of birth and death